MW01137115

MANKATO,

MINNESOTA;

Growing up in the '30s and '40s

By

Clayton Lagerquist

©Copyright, 2001, 2002, 2007 by Clayton Lagerquist
Walker, Minnesota

ISBN 978-1-4303-1320-5

Table of Contents

4

Introduction

I went to a professional meeting in Denver a few years ago where I heard a motivational speaker, Prof. Morris Massey, from the University of Colorado. His talk was famous and was entitled, "What you are, is where you were, when." He gave numerous examples of knowing how people would react to situations based only on how old they were and where they were raised.

I grew up in Mankato, Minnesota, in the 30's and 40's and it contributed to what I am. The way I was treated by my parents also had a big impact. These were the depression years and none of us was planned. The war had a huge impact on everything but we thought it was normal because we knew nothing different. The community as a whole indulged us and we felt safe in it.

There were many things about my dad that I didn't understand and maybe it was because I didn't know what it was like to be raised in his time.

My memories are quite good because I was so happy and told stories about my youth many times. I may be wrong about some things because I embellished some stories when I was young and now I can't remember which ones, but as someone once said, "If that ain't the way it was, that's the way it should have been."

Part 1
The Formative Years

School

It didn't seem like I would ever get old enough to go to school. Everyone else, it seemed, had someplace to go each day while I stayed at home. Mother took me to school when I was 4 years old thinking they would take me a year early but they said I wasn't ready. I think she was ready to have me gone for half a day.

When I finally got to go, I found school was a frightening and beautiful place. I never had a bad teacher although some were not very loving. They were all good disciplinarians so our time was never wasted. I was disappointed after the first day because they didn't teach me to read. I had been told I would be taught to read when I went to school. Kindergarten was not much of a challenge. We were always lining up to go somewhere and I didn't like to stand in line. Mother was called to a conference with my kindergarten teacher, Miss Radcliff, who wanted to know how to get me to stand in line. She said I was always one step to the side and if she pushed me back in line I would come out two steps. Mother said she had no advice because that was just the way I was.

We lined up once to go outside to look for the Easter Bunny. I must have said something derogatory because I was told to wait in the cloak hall. When the class was outside, the teacher's helper asked me to help her put jellybeans around the class room. When the class came back, they were told that the Easter Bunny had come while they were out looking for him. My brother, Bill, had long since told me there was no Tooth Fairy, Easter Bunny, or Santa Claus.

Once we were learning the difference between fruits and vegetables and I was bored because I knew them all. The teacher would go around the class and ask, "Is this a fruit or a vegetable?" When she got to me she said, "Tomato." I didn't know which it was and was so embarrassed. I knew all the rest. How could she pick that one for me? At Christmas time we made hot pad holders. We started with two paper plates and cut one in half. Then we put them face to face and sewed them together with yarn through holes we had punched. I think we colored or decorated them somehow to make them look like Christmas. I gave mine to Grandma and she hung it on the kitchen wall.

At the end of the year there was a special assembly of all the grades with kids from each class doing something on the stage. I drew a cat on an easel but told a story at the same time to describe the lines on the board. It went like this: Kit and Kat went over to someone's house (that was a straight line) but fell down a hole (that was a line for one side of a front leg) but he got back up out of the hole (that completed one front leg) etc. until the cat was done. I thought it was fun and had no fear of the stage.

On the school grounds we were learning more important things. Don Tate was showing me a switchblade knife when it went out of control and cut my finger. It was a small cut and healed without fuss.

Downtown

Many people didn't have cars so they relied on the city bus to take them around town. We had a car but Dad would take it to work so if Mother wanted to go downtown she would take the bus. The bus came every hour and went down 4th Street toward town. I went with Mother many times to shop downtown. I liked the dime stores best. There were three of them side by side. They were named Green's, Kresge's, and Woolworth's and they all carried pretty much the same merchandise. One of them had an automatic donut-making machine in the front that I used to watch. The dough was squeezed out of a double tube and would fall into the hot oil when it got big enough. The oil was moving slowly around in a circle and the donuts would fry on their way around. Half way around a mechanical spatula would turn them over. Mother didn't buy much there but she usually got a small bag of chocolate covered peanuts.

After one of the first days I went to school, Mother told me to go over to 4th Street and wait for her to come in the bus and we would go down town. She said she would have the bus driver stop the bus so I could get on. I usually went home on Broad Street with my friends but this time I went over to 4th Street. The bus came but went right on by. I couldn't see whether Mother was on it or not. I knew how to get home from there but I was pretty scared anyway. I worried about what might have happened to Mother. I ran all the way and when I got there she said she missed the bus. Ever since that day I hesitate when someone wants to meet me someplace at a certain time for fear they won't be there.

Games

When we weren't in school we would play games with other kids in the neighborhood. Jerry Neubert lived two doors away and I used to play with him. I remember being in his house several times. They had a hand pump in the kitchen for pumping cistern water to the sink. It was the first one I ever saw and asked all about it. I was in their house with a balloon once and got it too close to the gas range so it popped. Jerry's mother gave me a penny so I could buy another one. I thought she was very nice. Jerry's dad was a carpenter and we were told he could drive a nail into concrete. I didn't believe it.

The older kids in the neighborhood would teach the younger ones and sometimes make up rules to suit themselves during the game. Lorna Mae Menk lived next door and made up a lot of the rules. She invented a substitute for money that involved pins and jars of sand that had colored layers in them. I never understood that but others seemed to think it was all right. She was particularly nice to me. She was my brother's age and treated me like a little brother. Sometimes we would skip rope. She played hopscotch and jacks with me for hours. This must have made my Mother happy because I was always saying to her, "What's there to do?" When there were puffy clouds in the sky we would lie on our backs and see the many different animal shapes and faces that would come and go. Sometimes Mother would tell me to come in and take my nap right in the middle of these fun things. I used to hate that and resist until force was used.

Lorna Mae would take me to the local grocery store sometimes and hold my hand on the way. Her male friends used to holler to her that she had a boy friend but she didn't care. The store was a wonderful place to go because they had a showcase full of candy and an ice chest full of pop and a freezer with Popsicles. I thought I could sneak behind the showcase and help myself to some root beer barrels. I guess I wasn't the first to try that and I got caught. Lorna was told to watch me more closely and I thought it was strange that I wasn't held responsible. I decided that I could do anything I wanted because I was just a little kid. It was like when you are dreaming and know you are dreaming. You know you can do anything but hesitate to do it.

When I was a little older, I stole a fountain pen at the dime store. I brought it home but couldn't get it to work so I took it back and got a money refund.

On a summer evening we would play games like, Hide and Seek, Kick the Can, or Captain-May-I with anyone that would show up. Sometimes we would stomp on a can that had a top and bottom so they would stick to our shoes and clop, clop around like the sound of a horse. We also used to go to the creek to play. There was often someone else there. There was a rope tied to a tree and we could swing across the water. Too many times we got wet feet. Where the creek went under the road at Broad Street there was a nice big tunnel. We often played in there and it was a nice place to go to smoke if we didn't want anyone to see us.

Roller skating on the sidewalks was fun. We all had the roller skates that attached to our shoes with clamps in front that were tightened with a key (that was on a string around your neck) and a leather strap in back that went around the ankle.

Flying a kite sounded like an exciting thing to do so we got Dad to make one. Our first one was made out of newspaper and two sticks or dowels tied together in the form of a cross. We had rags for a tail and a big ball of string that was made from many small lengths of string tied together. We tried to fly it many times but we never got it to stay up in the air very long. If there wasn't enough wind we would run with the string and if there was too much wind it would do a loop and crash. I wish I could say we made better and better kites until we got it right but that didn't happen. I saw lots of other people with good flying kites but I never flew one.

Once Mother wanted to find something for me to do when I had been under her feet too long so she sent me out to pick May flowers. First she had to describe them and then tell me where to find them. It turned out that the pasture at Good Counsel Academy was the nearest place she knew about, so off I went. I came back with a whole handful but I'm not sure they were worth saving because I had been squeezing them for so long. She seemed so happy I picked them several times after that.

In the summer when it was really hot we would sometimes go for a ride in Dad's car to cool off. We were allowed to hold toy airplanes out the window so we could feel the wind on the wings pushing the planes up and down. I lost one that way. We stopped and looked along the ditch but couldn't find it. Occasionally we even stopped at a root beer stand to get the free 'baby' root beer for us kids.

In the winter we would try to ski with those skis that had only a leather strap across the toe. We would pile snow high enough in the yard to have a slope.

Bill Skiing Down 'our' Hill

Sometimes we would walk to the Good Counsel Academy hill and ski or sled all day. My sled ran into a tree

on that hill once and I got a bad nosebleed because I was lying on my stomach with my nose out front. I ran all the way home dripping blood. Other times we just built forts and threw snowballs at each other. Getting dressed and undressed for these events was a major undertaking.

The house was cold in the morning until Dad got the fire going again. He would shake out the ashes (we could hear that all through the house), put some new coal in and open a damper. If we got to sleep late, the heat would come up the registers and we could stand by them as we dressed. When we dressed before it got warm we often dressed under the covers. The hardest part was getting the garter belt on right side up and not backwards. The garter belt was needed to hold up the long stockings.

If it was too cold to play outside, there was the radio. Jack Armstrong was a favorite, but there were many good radio shows for kids. Advertisers often used a gimmick to sell their products and Wheaties box tops were used for all sorts of prizes. Mother usually had 6 or 8 boxes of Wheaties in the cupboard with their tops gone. Once we got pedometers that clipped to our belt and measured how far we had walked. Needless to say we did an awful lot of unnecessary walking. We had other indoor games with marbles. We would sit on the floor at opposite ends of a room with our legs apart. Then we would put a marble in front of us and the other one would roll a marble toward it trying to hit it. If they hit the roller got both marbles, otherwise it went to the other player. Of course, this game was not for 'keeps'; it was for 'funs'.

Sometimes we played solitaire with worn-out cards. We only knew one game so we played it over and over.

I followed Bill everywhere but I was never welcome. He wanted to play with his friends and I wasn't big enough. He tried everything including hitting my arm in the same place until it was sore all the time. When he did that I would swear at him and he would tell Mother. I always got scolded for that.

I got a lot of hand-me-down clothes from Bill including shoes. They were stored in a way that I could see which ones I was going to get next. I remember mostly the scandals that were lined up for the next three years. Tennis shoes were never on the list of things to get. They were the cloth and rubber high tops with the circle of rubber protecting the cloth where the bone on the outside of the foot would cause undo wear. Tennis shoes always wore out before they were outgrown and usually were smelly and rotten from getting wet.

When Ann was expected, I was told by my mother that I was soon not going to be the baby of the family. I thought that was fine but I guess she thought I would be jealous. She probably read that somewhere because she was a real reader. The night Ann was born a friend of my dad's came to stay with us. I think his name was Bruno Bladel. He and Dad had made a duck boat together. We didn't get to see Ann for 10 days because it was customary to keep the mother and baby that long in the hospital. When they did come home, I found out how much work a baby was. Mother never complained but when Ann was older Mother did say, "I'll never learn how to cut a pint of ice cream into 5 parts." I was curious enough about the new baby to be right there for everything. The bathinette with it's natural rubber smell, and the powder with it's smell were new to me. The diapers were all done by hand except for the final wash. Ann was a perfect baby and made it possible for Mother to manage the rest of our needs as best she could. Dad even seemed to be around the house more.

Ann and Janice

Ann was 6 years younger than I and 9 years younger than Bill. She wasn't part of our games, jobs, or school so she isn't mentioned often in my remembrances of my younger days. She was more of a center of our doting and we defended her like she was a personal possession. When she was first learning to talk she called Dad 'Dad' and me 'Daddy' so we straightened her out on that and then she called me Dee Dee. Mother picked up on that and she called me Dee Dee for many years.

Before 3 Years Old

I can remember many things before I was old enough to go to school. My very first recollections are like a single frame taken out of a roll of movie film. My kiddy car was one thing that I liked but I wondered why my feet weren't allowed to touch the ground and why all those beads were on a rod in such a way that they couldn't be rearranged. What was the fun of pushing them back and forth.

I used to get a bath in the kitchen sink when I was at my grandmother's. I couldn't have been very big. I also had a toy that was on a string and I could sit in a highchair and dangle it to the floor. It was a red car with huge rubber tires so it worked upside down as well as right-side up. I saw an old one in an antique store not too long ago but the rubber was bad so I didn't get it. I used to have a pink rabbit with wires in his ears to hold them up. I was a little confused by him because I wasn't sure if he was alive or not.

Clayt and the Pink Rabbit

I'm not sure what the first recollections of my mother were but she was always there like a security blanket. She always said, "Everything will turn out all right." I remember her rocking me to sleep every night. She used to sing to me, and one of her favorite songs was, "You take the high road and I'll take the low road and I'll be in Scotland afore ye." I used to try to picture these two roads but without success. She explained everything in great detail, like crossing the street you look left, then right, then left again - even if there is not a car in sight. She used to brush my hair 100 strokes a day to 'train' it. My scalp was sore for months. She counted out loud so I would learn my numbers. She also went over the alphabet out loud and I learned that except I thought *lmnop* was one letter. She preferred to be called Mother and would not answer to Ma. She never had a job outside of the house because it was a full time job around the house without any of our present day labor saving devices. Laundry took all day Monday. Ironing took all day Tuesday because it included starching my dad's white shirts. Cooking, washing dishes and sewing took the rest of the time. Notice there was no time for cleaning or dusting. I thought it was normal to have dust balls under the bed and dust so deep in the cold air registers that when marbles would fall in them, they were lost. The cold air registers were about 2ft x 3ft with wooden grates over them so they collected a lot of marbles.

I used to 'help' my mother with everything. When she made fudge, I would clean the pan. When she sewed, I would sit on the floor by the treadle machine and marvel at how the treadle motion was converted to a round and round motion by the device that looked like the arms and shoulders of a man with no head. In the kitchen I walked under the breadboard and she said I wouldn't be able to do that much longer. Getting taller was of great interest to everyone. Each time we would go to Minneapolis, Mildred would make us stand by the wall in her room and she would mark how tall we were on the wallpaper and see how much we had grown. I even had growing pains in my legs and took aspirin to take the pain away. It always took one hour. Sometimes, when I wasn't helping Mother, I would ride my rocking horse in the living room. It wasn't a horse on rockers but rather like a double leaf spring with a seat on it that could be pumped up and down. I would stare at the picture on the wall with the fat ladies sitting around a pool and pump up and down until I felt like I wasn't even there. If I pumped hard enough I would come off the seat each time it got to the top. When I got tired I would push two stuffed chairs together, put a blanket over the arms and crawl in for a nap.

The first time I went up the stairs by alternating my feet was a proud moment. Of course, I still had my hand on the stairs for balance but it seemed like an eternity that I had been going up one foot first and then bringing the other foot even with it before tackling the next step. I learned this coming up from the basement. At the top of the stairs there was a place where the dry dog food was kept. It smelled so good I used to eat a biscuit once in a while but I didn't tell anyone. When I didn't get my way I would lie down and hold my breath. I thought they would worry about me dying but they knew better so I had to resort to crying and sobbing. I could sob for hours.

We had a milkman that came every day. He would let himself in the side door by the kitchen and take the empty bottles and leave full ones. Mother was usually there and he would try to sell her something else. She paid with coupons. He always smelled like Spearmint gum and his name was Red. One day he said to me, "What cha doin, Ayton?" I am reported to have said, "Ayton eatin'." My mother started calling me Ayton after that. The milk used to separate with the cream coming to the top. We had a little spoon that fit down to the neck of the bottle so we could pour off the cream.

At some point I learned to tie my own shoes, first with one bow, then with two. That seemed like a big milestone.

Clayt and the Trike

Riding my trike was great fun. I called it *my* trike but actually it was Bill's trike first and Ann's trike later. I even rode it in the house. I would go round and round the dining room table as evidenced by the deep scratches on the legs. They came from my axle when I cut the corner too sharply. Even putting one foot on the back of the trike and pushing with the other was better than the scooter I had. I was so excited when I learned to tell time and luckily all the clocks had numbers on them.

Once a big kid from across the street ran over me on my trike with his bike and my dad saw it. He took out after that kid and brought him in our front porch where he shook him up pretty good. I wasn't hurt but watched the confrontation closely. When it was over he sent the kid home. Mother was there and said, "You tore his shirt and that is probably the only one he has." I think the kid's last name was Barnes and they were really poor. I wouldn't have remembered this incident if I hadn't felt so sorry for him. I always felt too much emotion. I was obsessed with things I couldn't have; I felt sorry for people that were poor; and I didn't have to be taught to be nice to animals. I came into this world feeling this way and I didn't think it was a blessing because it always made me feel bad. I had to learn how to cry without showing it.

Mother had to teach me some things, however. I caught a bird in my hand when it was trying to get out of the garage window. My heart was going a hundred miles an hour when I showed it to Mother. She said, "Let it go; birds aren't happy unless they are free and we can't enjoy them unless they are happy." So I let it go. It flew to the top of a nearby tree and sang to us. I could see that she was right.

I was pretty curious about everything. I had been warned so many times to be careful not to fall down the stairs that I decided to find out how bad it was. I went to the top of the stairs and just fell forward. When I got to the bottom the door was shut and I smacked into it pretty hard. Mother came running and got me quieted down before she saw that I had a big swollen knob on my forehead. I could feel it too. She had read somewhere that it was best to put something cold on a bump like that so she went to the kitchen and got a silver knife because we didn't have ice cubes. When I saw her coming with the knife I panicked because I thought she intended to cut off the knob.

I wondered about how the lamps worked; what made the lights come on? Electricity was pretty expensive so we didn't have bulbs in all of the sockets. There was room for two light bulbs in the floor lamp but it only had one. It screwed into a socket that looked like a candle complete with the drippings. I had been warned many times but I stuck my finger down the socket. Needless to say I didn't do it twice.

Grandma and Grandpa

I was sent to live with my grandparents in Minneapolis during the spring of 1936. I didn't know the reason at the time, but it was because both my brother, Bill, and my mother were in the hospital with mastoid operations. This was an ear infection that spreads to the bone behind the ear. Without antibiotics, it was a serious condition that could lead to death if it spread to the brain cavity. I visited them in the hospital a couple of times but didn't know how serious it was. My dad had his hands full so I was taken to my grandparents to live.

Grandma and Grandpa

It was a wonderful time for me. My grandparent's thought I could do no wrong and that was fine with me. I remember a great deal about that spring which may sound surprising because I had only turned three years old that March. Actually, I remember quite a few things before that, including my third birthday.

One of the first things that happened to me wasn't much fun, however. My brother came down with scarlet fever while he was in the hospital, so I was taken to a doctor to get a series of shots to help prevent me from getting it. After the first shot I asked if they could use a duller needle. I wouldn't have remembered this but my grandparents told everyone what I had said. On one of the trips to get a shot, Grandpa locked the keys in the car and had to take the streetcar home to get another set of keys. I waited in the doctor's office probably because they wanted me to stay long enough to make sure there was no reaction to the shot.

Bill and Clayt

Grandpa had a 1935 Chevy and he took me everywhere in it. We went to Monkey Island at Como Park, the Museum of Natural History at the University, the Ford assembly plant, the water treatment plant on the Mississippi River, to visit relatives in Anoka, to a circus, and I'm sure many other places. Many times Grandma would think of things for us to do and Grandpa would do it. This sounds a little like he was hen-pecked but he had a reputation of being such a nice guy that he probably welcomed the suggestions. He even took me to his work once and let me play with a stamp that could be adjusted for different dates.

Anyway, they treated me like an adult and talked to me about everything. They told me I could do anything I wanted to do with my life. I think they expected me to be some sort of a world leader because they warned me about Germany and Russia. They said a war was coming. Once when we drove past an auto junkyard, Grandpa told me that the junk dealers were saving the steel to sell when the war started. We also rode the streetcar some. When I asked why the blacks (called Negroes then) were all standing outside at the rear of the streetcar, he told me they often brought live chickens home so they couldn't sit inside. I accepted that and was later shocked to learn that they had to stay at the rear even if they had no chickens and there were plenty of seats up front. We didn't have blacks in Mankato so this was all new to me. I liked the streetcars and watched the drivers move the handle in a circular motion to go ahead or stop. They had lots of acceleration and a cowcatcher out in front.

The circus wasn't as thrilling as they told me it would be. I never could see what was suppose to be funny about the clowns. I liked the elephants and we were allowed to feed them peanuts before the show. A little car drove to the center of the ring and midgets started to get out. I couldn't figure out how they got so many people in that little car. The trapeze artists made it look so easy I wasn't thrilled. The toilet was nothing but a long trench; not very private.

Monkey Island at Como Park was one of my favorites. I watched the monkeys at length and am reported to have said to Grandpa, "Don't you wish you were a monkey?" I was also taken for a ride on a Carousel but they gave me a horse that didn't go up and down. I liked the music but it made me dizzy to look out at the people as they went by.

Cotton candy always looked good to me but I was told it was impossible to eat without making a sticky mess. So I never got any.

I saw the 1936 Fords come off the end of the assembly line. A guy would put gas in them and drive them away. They talked about having their own glass plant and how the glass was made from sand. That was hard to believe. I didn't understand how the water treatment plant worked but I was surprised that the tap water came from the river. I was glad Grandpa would drive to a nearby park with gallon jugs to get our drinking water from a hand-operated pump.

The Museum of Natural History was mostly stuffed animals and I had a hard time figuring out whether they were dead or alive. Many years later when I worked at the University, I went over there to see if my memory was correct. It was just as I had remembered.

My grandparent's house seemed huge to me. It was three stories tall and looked like most of the other houses in the neighborhood that were built around 1915. It was only 32 blocks north of down town Minneapolis but was in the suburbs. There were still a few vacant lots in their block.[*]

A porch ran across the whole front of the house. The mailbox was in there and the mailman used come in every day and talk to me if I was there. One side had no furniture but the other side had a couple of chairs and a wonderful swing. I spent a lot of time in that swing. When I would lie down I could smell the cushions. I would put my

---

*Grandmother wrote a short autobiography that included the history of building this house.

feet out the end and touch the wall so I could give it a little push so the swing would go side to side. That used to get me into trouble when I pushed too hard and bumped the house. When I did that during Grandma's nap time she was especially upset.

Clayt at Grandpa's

From the porch one would enter the house through a door that led to a short hall and then another door to the house. The door from the hall led to an entryway that had a two-story ceiling that allowed an open stairs to the second floor. This room had a piano and a hall tree complete with umbrellas and overshoes under the seat. To the left as you came in there were double pocket doors (that slid into the wall) leading to the living room.

This room was closed off some of the time. It did contain the radio, however, and it was turned on every day to listen to the news.

The Radio, Clayt, and Bill

I think it was Gabriel Heater that gave the news. I thought the radio had only one station. If you went straight ahead from the entrance hall past the living room doors and the stairway you would find the kitchen. It was big. The dining room was to the left of the kitchen and connected to the living room. The kitchen had lots of cabinets and bins for flour and sugar. A mouse came out of one of these bins once and upset my grandmother.

There was a pantry with a big cylindrical box of popped popcorn in it and there was a loud clock on the wall of the kitchen that had to be wound each night.

The upstairs was like a box with a hall going down the middle. There were 4 bedrooms and a bath. The bath was at the end of the hall. The bedroom at the other end of the hall wasn't used as a bedroom. I don't think it even had a bed in it. There was also a door to the stairs that led to the attic. The attic was wonderful, partly because I wasn't allowed to go up there alone, so, of course, I never did. The walls were not finished and it smelled like an attic. It was very hot and contained things in storage. There were lots of National Geographics and boxes of clothes. There was even a sword hanging on the wall.

My grandparents both came from Sweden when they were very young so they spoke Swedish as their first language. They spoke it whenever they didn't want me to understand them. Sometimes I could, however. I could not detect an accent in their English. My grandfather went only through the third grade in school and I assume about the same for my grandmother. They were both self educated, however, and competed in a world of the educated. My grandfather retired as an office manager for the State of Minnesota's Grain and Warehouse Commission. My Great Aunt Mildred also worked there as a secretary. She was my grandmother's half sister. She was raised with my dad and uncle as though she was a big sister. I thought she was great until my brother pointed out all her flaws. The three of them, Grandpa, Grandma, and Mildred, treated me like a new toy. They often had games for me like, dropping clothespins into a bottle over the back of a chair or fishing with a pole and string over a sheet (one of them would be behind the sheet and put little wooden fish on my string). I never did think this was exciting but I pretended anyway so they would feel good. They also let me 'plink' on the piano and look at stereoscopic pictures.

Grandpa shaved with a straight edge razor that he sharpened on a leather strop. I couldn't figure out how that made it sharp and I still wonder about it. I would watch him with interest so he got out a box of brand new safety razors for me to play with. The handles unscrewed and there was a piece of cardboard where the blade would fit. I took them apart put them together and pretended to shave with them. I don't know why he had so many new ones.

Grandma 'let' me dust and I didn't mind because she was so complimentary to me when I finished. The best part was the sides of the stairs between the carpet and the balusters. I could spend an hour doing that justice.

They had a visitor, a distant relative, from Sweden that summer and she was a nurse. She came in handy because I had developed a sore on my heel where the shoes rubbed. She put on new gauze bandages every day. It was nice to have my own nurse.

I spent a lot of time in the swing watching the cars go by on Lyndale Avenue. At the time I thought the street was a long way away. I enjoyed the cars day and night because it kept me from getting too lonesome. Nights were especially bad when everyone else was asleep. One day I saw a hook and ladder fire engine come around the corner at 33rd and Lyndale and smash into a parked car. It was such a long truck that there was a fellow steering the back wheels separately but he didn't adjust to the corner fast enough.

I played records on their wind up Victrola. I would peek into the slats on the front to try to figure out what made the sounds in there. They had a comedy record by the Two Black Crows. They were comedians and would tell stories including these two: "Let's measure the two horses to see if we can tell them apart by their size -- and sure enough the black one was 3 inches taller than the white one." And "Let's meet down by the store. If I get there first I'll draw a line on the sidewalk and if you get there first, you can erase it."

I was allowed to walk to the grocery store alone to get an item or two for Grandmother. The store was only a half a block away but it was across the street. This was Lyndale Avenue and it was busy even then. I had to learn their phone number before I could go. It was Ch(erry) 6916. I learned it well. I think they watched the whole time and even called neighbors to watch me go by and I'm sure they called the store. There was a stop and go sign at the corner but not like the lights we have today. Instead it was metal box in the middle of the street that had a mechanical movement inside. The center part would rotate and display either stop or go. I was too young to read but they taught me the difference between stop and go the same way I learned hot and cold. They also let me go around the block as long as I didn't cross any streets. The blocks seemed bigger than they are now and it was scary to be that far from home. I used to count my way around. 1, 2, 3, 4, there I can see the house. All this was fine until I was visiting Uncle Irving and Aunt Rufine's house. I asked Aunt Rufine if I could go around the block because I knew how. What I didn't know was that they lived on a 5 cornered block. When I got to 4 and couldn't see their house, I panicked and ran until I saw it. I didn't know what happened but I didn't want to try again. Uncle Irving and Aunt Rufine were the only close relatives we had until their daughter, Janice, was born in 1938. Grandpa had a brother and sister that lived down on the corner at 33rd Avenue. His name was Alfred and hers was Hilda. Hilda was married to Axel Johnson but Alfred never married. We saw them quite a bit when we would go to Minneapolis to visit.

My grandparents were pillars of the church and there was always some function to go to. Often there was a picnic associated with it. Grandma would fill up the picnic box that Grandpa made with the space for the two Stanley thermos bottles. There were always potato salad and sandwiches. The picnic planners put a bunch of coins in a pile of sand and let the kids dig for them. I didn't find any but did get a lot of sand in my clothes. We went to church often and I would concentrate on the huge light fixtures that hung by chains from the tall ceiling. I was afraid they would fall down. Grandma taught me to say my prayers at night and I worried about the part where I said, "If I should die before I wake." I thought there was a good chance that might happen and I was afraid to die. I told my grandparents that I was glad they were old and I was new. I didn't know that was funny until I heard them telling their friends.

We all drove to Mankato to visit my mother and brother in the hospital. They were in bed but looked all right to me. I had just learned to whistle and was reminded many times that it wasn't permissible to whistle in the hospital.

They even took me to a dentist. There was nothing wrong but I think they wanted me to be able to go to a dentist without worry. Both of them had false teeth and they showed me how they took them out at night and put them in a glass of water. I was very impressed, especially when they sucked in their cheeks.

When we went to Anoka to visit relatives, it was shortly after the town had been hit by a tornado. I heard our relatives lost a barn and some nice trotting horses. There was much talk about all the freak things that happened but I was stunned when they said the water was blown out of the river and one could see the deadheads (sunken logs) on the bottom. I didn't know what a deadhead was but I could picture some pretty horrible things.

We visited Minneapolis many times before and after that spring but my brother was always there on these other visits so I remember them differently.

On the way to the basement, there was a landing where the stairs turned. We sat on this landing and watched grandpa in his workshop just below. He made things out of wood. He had hand chisels and made a likeness of Bill and me from a photograph. He had a wood lathe and made wheels on it for a couple of soapbox cars.

Bill and Clayt in Soapbox Cars

Grandpa would play games with us by the hour. We played checkers, Chinese checkers, pick up sticks, and a game he made. It was a board with calendar numbers pasted on it with a nail at each number. We would throw jar rings at it and get credit for the number where the ring hung on a nail. There was a model airplane shop on Lowry Avenue right by our alley so we made some model airplanes and found out it doesn't work to stretch the paper by drying the wet part in the oven. The paper would shrink so much that it would twist the part. There was an older kid next door that made beautiful model airplanes including a glider with a 5ft. wing span. He also had pigeons by the garage and a dog that was always kept in a pen.

Grandpa had tamed a squirrel by feeding it and we were allowed to hold peanuts up on our shoulder so the squirrel would climb up our clothes and sit on our shoulder while he ate the peanuts.

Bill told me it would be all right to pee in the corner of Grandpa's garage so I did it several times. Grandpa soon told me not to do it anymore and I wondered how he knew.

Roll-top Desk

I'm not sure when I first saw the big oak desk but I wasn't very old. It belonged to Charles Swanson and it was his pride and joy. He took me by the hand one day and led me to his office where it was sitting under a huge moose head. The desk looked even bigger than it was because I was so small. He showed me the many drawers and cubbyholes. He didn't know that it would be mine one day. The Swanson's owned a big brickyard in north Minneapolis just across the river from my grandparents. The big house and grounds were a part of the acreage devoted to the business. It was like a park and totally secluded. Our family had several ties with the Swanson's starting with Grandpa's sister, Emma, who lived with them and was the cook, companion and what ever else she could do. She lived there all her life starting when she was a small girl. I guess this was a common practice but seemed strange to me. She was a good looking young girl from her pictures but never got married. Other members of our family had worked there also including Mildred's father who did the books using the big desk. Our family was often invited to the Swanson's during holidays and was treated like family.

Mankato

In spite of all the pampering I got in Minneapolis I was anxious to get back to Mankato. I didn't like Minneapolis because it was too big, too flat, and too busy.

I liked the size of Mankato at about 15,000 to 20,000. Wherever we lived in town it was only a few blocks to the edge of town and the countryside that I loved. Mankato was built in a river valley so it was surrounded by hills 200 ft. high that were covered with mature hardwood trees. That gave it a cozy feeling. Throughout my youth I wondered how the river could have been a mile wide at some time in the past and why the earth had dried up so much. There were also ravines coming in to the valley that were formed by rivers almost as big as the main one that is now called the Minnesota River. I read somewhere that in prehistoric times this huge river was the outlet of Lake Agessiz and was called the River Warren. Of course that's just what some historian called it. It was also called the St. Peter or Pierre River by the first fur traders. Whatever it's name, it comes across Minnesota from the northwest and takes a sharp turn at Mankato before it goes north northeast to Minneapolis where it joins the Mississippi. The Blue Earth River joins the Minnesota right at the bend. Since the streets of Mankato were laid out along the curving river, it was confusing to me when I tried to keep track of north and south. Even the streets where I first remember living went northeast and southwest instead of north and south like I thought they did.

The weather controlled all of our activities. The only thing for sure about the weather in Minnesota was that it would be too hot sometimes in the summer and too cold sometimes in the winter. Year-to-year variations were hard to predict. One year it wasn't cold enough at Christmas to make ice at the skating rink. Of the four seasons, only spring was bad in my mind. It was cold, wet, rainy, muddy, overcast, and lasted forever.

Waiting for things to improve during spring involved looking for the first robin to arrive. They seemed to know something that we didn't. When they would first appear Mother would say that the early bird gets the worm. It didn't make sense to me because there was plenty of worms for all the birds.

Fall was the best but it didn't last very long. It was the time of year to be out in the country as much as possible but even in town it was great. We would make big piles of leaves and jump into them and sometimes cover up with them. When someone burned them in the gutter, the smell was wonderful.

The hot part of the summer was unbearable because there never was a breeze and, of course, no air conditioners. The town was down in a hollow and all the trees were mature and almost touched each other in the middle of the street. When it got over 100 degrees, people would begin to come out of their houses and sit on their front steps.

During the bitter cold days of winter, cars wouldn't start, the windows would frost over, walking anywhere was a bitter experience, and skating wasn't even any fun. All activities were done indoors. Some years there was so much snow that there was no place to put it. Shoveling was all by hand and the wind might put it right back after the shoveling.

In the coldest part of the winter, the windows would frost over completely so we couldn't see out. We would melt away some of it with our hand to see out and when it frosted over again, our hand print would show. Sometimes we blew on it to melt a nice circle to look through. We had storm windows but they didn't work on the coldest days. In the spring, the storm windows would freeze shut from the melting and freezing of the frost between the windows so we would pour warm water in the sill to open them so things could dry out.

When the snow melted in the spring it revealed layer after layer of dirty snow from the coal furnaces. Sometimes the spring was so slow to come, the weather turned to summertime without spring.

The House on Fourth Street

My life as a youngster seems segmented by the houses where I lived. Houses were very important because I associate my activities with them.

The house on North 4th Street is the first one I remember. It was a two-bedroom bungalow with another bedroom upstairs in the front. The rest of the upstairs was unfinished except it had walls down either side that made sort of a hall down the middle. There was storage space on either side of the wall. Bill would tell me of all the things that lived there. For a while we slept up there when Ann was born so I wasted no time getting from the top of the stairs to the bedroom in case one of those things would come out. There was no bathroom up there so we had a chamber pot under the bed. There was no rug.

It was a nice house and had all the modern conveniences, such as a refrigerator and hot water. The refrigerator had a freezer compartment, but it only held one pint of ice cream. Many others in our block had iceboxes so in the summer we would follow the iceman and eat chips of ice that he shaved off the blocks. We were told not to eat the ice because it was dirty but it looked clean to us. We didn't know that it was cut right out of the river by Sibley Park. The ice man knew how much ice each house wanted because they would rotate a card in the window until the number of pounds they wanted would be on the top –- 25, 50, 75, or 100.

The hot water worked only when we lit the gas fire in the hot water tank so taking a bath meant planning ahead. The fire was lit under a coil that was about two feet high and eight inches in diameter. The water flowing through the coil would get hot but if it weren't used right away it would boil. If we heard the hot water heater bumping it was time to turn off the flame and run the bath. The water that first came was too hot but there wasn't much of it so we would run all the hot water first and then cool it off with the water that came next.

There was a drive way in the front of the house. There were bushes at the end of the driveway that had white flowers that smelled so nice. I used to pick them and carry them around.

There was an empty lot next door that belonged to the people on the corner. It was used for a huge garden. It was fun to watch the team of horses do the plowing in the spring. The only thing I ate from their garden was the ground cherries. We had plenty of room to put in a garden but Dad chose to mow it all instead. We had raspberry and gooseberry bushes on either side all the way back to the alley. The garage was out by the alley. There were hollyhocks by the garage and I learned not to play with them after they went to seed because all those seeds would go down my neck. I liked the alley and played there a lot. This is where we played hopscotch and marbles.

We had a nice tree in front of the house that was ideal for climbing. We went up it so often that the bark was nearly worn off the first branch. There was room for several kids up there at a time. I fell out of that tree once and landed on my back. It knocked all the wind out of me. Mother must have been watching because she got there in a flash and blew air into my mouth. She must have read that somewhere.

When I lived on 4th Street my neighborhood was confined to about 3 blocks in each direction. Even though I could have gone three blocks west, I never did it alone because I was afraid of the kids on Second Street. With that range, however, I could get to school, Tourtellotte Park and pool, Good Counsel Academy, the creek, and the hill on the south side of Thompson Ravine Road. It was on this hill that some of the older kids dug underground shacks. I guess it is every boy's desire to have a secret place to go and to hide things. The hill was the site of an old cemetery and there was talk about what was found digging in these places.

I used this hill to throw rocks from a sling shot that I twirled around my head. I never knew for sure which way the rocks would go so I went up there so I couldn't damage anything. The rocks would go a long way.

Mother complained that the kitchen was too hot in the summer so she had Dad plant a tree that would give it some shade. She said, "It probably won't do me any good, but someday it will help someone."

I was sick on the eve of my third birthday. I was sick a lot with all those horrible childhood diseases and colds. When I got sick, I really got sick and Mother's treatments didn't help. I always got an enema no matter what the problem was. Sometimes I would have to sit with my feet in a pail of hot water. So hot, I couldn't put my feet in for a long time. Then there was the stuff that was put around my neck. First a rag soaked in cold water, then several layers of wool rags. On my chest she would put a big smear of Vick's Vapor Rub or something that smelled even worse. Sometimes I got a mustard plaster on my chest. I was usually in bed for days. When I could start eating again I got milk toast with sugar on it. Once when I got up after a long sickness, I looked in the mirror and was shocked. I looked so skinny even my teeth looked like they had spread apart. Mother used to try to prevent sickness by giving us cod liver oil. There was something about that that was worse than getting sick.

My third birthday was something I had looked forward to for a long time. I even said to myself, "It's been forever since I had a birthday." In the middle of the night I went down the hall to my folk's room, woke them up and asked if I could open a present early because I was sick. They agreed and I opened the package from Minneapolis. In it there was a red box with figurines in it. I don't know what they represented but I loved the box. It had a cover that was split with one third of the top that opened separately from the other two thirds. I loved it like I loved my red handled scissors. I also loved eyeglasses and wanted to be able to wear them. I felt a passion for objects like they were alive. Longing for things was also blown out of proportion. I always wanted something but I wanted a watch so badly that I would stare at the page of watches in the Sears Catalog until I knew every face there.

New Car

Mother in the 1936 Ford

A family's car was important. Not just for the transportation but for the prestige it brought. It didn't matter what your house looked like but everyone knew what kind of car you had. Of course, no one had two. Dad bought a brand new 1936 Ford and we thought it was great. Before we got the new one we had a Model A. Taking a trip in the Model A was a project because it was so cold inside we had to be all bundled up. The radiator used to boil over frequently and fill the inside with a wonderful smell of alcohol. Sitting in the back seat of a car in winter was not much fun. There was no heater back there and the cold air would leak in around the doors. We tried everything to keep our feet warm but nothing worked. Our folks would repeatedly say, "Are your feet cold?" We would answer, "No." We wondered why they asked because our feet were always cold. The back seat in the new car wasn't much warmer, but it had a lot of other advantages. When I was up front I didn't always sit in the seat but was allowed to stand on the front floor and look out.

When Dad heard that the Brewery in St. Peter was burning we drove over there as fast as the car would go. He told people that it went 90 but I doubt that. I watched very carefully how he drove it. At least the way he used the gas, the clutch, and the shift lever. Even the starter button was in a funny place on the floor.

Bill and I used to compare it to Grandpa's Chevy and decided the Ford was so much better. The gas pedal and the clutch pedal were so much easier to push.

This car was used to take us to Mission Lake in spite of the tiny 'lump trunk' that it had.

Grandma and Grandpa used to visit us often. When they were expected, I would get so excited that time would stand still and I would drive my folks crazy asking , "When are they going to get here"? Once Dad took me in the car to the highway where we could sit and wait for them. I think he was always pretty anxious to see them too.

When I was about 5 years old, my grandparents gave each of their grandchildren a $500 church bond. That was a lot of money to give away then and they weren't rich. They didn't even have health insurance and were getting old enough to worry about it. The bonds paid 2% interest that was paid by clipping a coupon. The interest went into the savings account. That much money would have bought all the things I wanted while growing up but Dad wouldn't let us spend any of it. It became more of a sore spot than a gift. I couldn't figure out why they didn't give it to Dad. He could have used it. I know he had to borrow lots of money to pay the hospital bill that Mother and Bill had 2 years earlier. If it was to be used for education or something special, they still could have given it to Dad to hold. I begged to spend some on skis, skates, bikes, and everything else but he held out until I was a senior in college when I used it for a car.

Aunt Mina

Aunt Mina, Bill & Clayt 1938

My Aunt Mina died on my 5th birthday and I waited outside for Dad to come home so I could tell him. Mother was pretty broken up. She was only 32 years old at the time Aunt Mina died. Mother was raised by her Aunt Mina and Uncle John Ecke. Her folks were divorced shortly after she was born and she lived with her dad for a while but soon his sister, Mina, took Mom to raise. Her dad's name was Frank Christensen, so Mother was christened Florence Christensen. I visited Aunt Mina and Uncle John a few times in Minneapolis where they lived near the railroad track. I watched the passenger trains go by about a half a block away. Uncle John was a blacksmith and it was said he would get pretty drunk on his home made beer. Supposedly he passed out and got wedged under the running board of his car. Aunt Mina couldn't get him out so she just left him there in the garage until he woke up. He made an ice chisel and two big iron magnets that he gave to Dad. The magnets were so strong that I couldn't hold them together backwards. Aunt Mina would come to Mankato by Greyhound bus to stay with us when mother needed help. She came in the winter once and when she got back home she found Uncle John sitting in an overcoat in a cold house. The fire had gone out and he didn't restart it because that was her job.

Bill and Clayt with New Watches

Uncle John surprised Bill and me by giving us wristwatches. I wonder how he knew how much I wanted one and for a change I didn't have to wait 3 years after Bill got something before I got one.

Mother's real mother married a well-to-do Canadian but when he died young, she was left with nothing because of Canadian law. She came back to this country but died in her early 50's of a stroke. Uncle John gave up and died shortly after Aunt Mina. Mother got nothing of their estate because she didn't step forward and ask for it. She said later that she thought Aunt Mina had an illegitimate child before she met Uncle John. Mother thought this child would step forward but it didn't happen so a court appointed lawyer got the property for closing the estate.

Vacations

Vacation to me meant only one thing -- the lake. Dad got two weeks vacation each year and he would use one for hunting and one at the lake. Each year we went up north to Mission Lake to stay at Pine Shores Resort.

Our family, Mildred, and Mina

This was also the favorite lake of my uncle and aunt and my grandparents. Sometimes we were all there together. Aunt Mina was even invited sometimes. Part of the good memories of these vacations was the good mood that would come over my dad. He was all smiles and patient with us. He didn't always give us our way but that is understandable. We always wanted to go fishing with him but if my grandfather and Uncle Irving were there, there wasn't room in the boat. When I couldn't go with them I would often fish from shore. I never caught anything this way and it's no surprise because I could only get my line out about a foot from shore were it was about 6 inches deep. They made exceptions sometimes if there was no wind and I sat in the front seat with the anchor. I never wanted to quit fishing once I got out there and was accused of saying, "I just had a bite," when someone suggested we go back. None of us could swim very well and life jackets were not used so we were very cautious. The boats were small but everyone was happy that Rosti, the owner of the Resort, supplied us with 'round bottom' boats. No one was allowed to stand up in the boat and we rowed wherever we went.

Round Bottom Boat

Catching fish was wonderful. It is hard to describe the excitement that I felt just thinking about it. Usually we caught pan fish with drop lines or cane poles. It was hard to bring in a big bluegill or crappie with a long cane pole. There was no shortage of these fish either. The crappies would school near the surface and show us their fins above the water. This happened almost every evening after supper.

Sometimes we would cut up a perch to use the meat for bait but usually we fished with minnows that Rosti would provide free. He would seine them with a net in front of the resort and put them in a big minnow box that was in about 4 feet of water. Sometimes we would fish for northern pike using small perch for bait.

Northerns

Bill caught a 14 pounder once and had his picture in the paper. I think Grandpa helped him get the fish in the boat. By then we were using rods and reels. The line was made of cotton and it had to be dried each time it was used. We would have two nails in the cabin and wind the line around them each night.

Bill and his 14 pound Northern

At some point, Dad got a little outboard motor. It was an Evenrude Elto with about 1 1/4 horsepower. It didn't say on the motor. It opened up other parts of the lake and even Lower Mission Lake that was connected by way of a narrow waterway.

Swimming was also a great joy. We always argued about whether the water was warm enough. We wore rubber bathing caps (probably because of the ear infections that Mother and Bill had). The rubber had a distinctive smell and every once in a while I smell that kind of rubber and remember those caps. We weren't allowed to go swimming for an hour after eating for fear of cramps but neither of us could swim so that didn't make too much sense to us.

1936 after Bill's surgery

We got to stay two weeks once or twice when we would go up with Grandpa and Grandma for a week and then Mom and Dad would come the next week.

Dad in his Fishing Clothes

The cabins were all hand made by Rosti so they had a lot in common. They all had a fireplace made of river rock cemented together. They also had an icebox that could be filled with ice from the outside. It was said that if he saw liquor or beer in the icebox, you wouldn't be able to get a reservation for next year. They didn't have running water so we used an outhouse and drank water from a bucket that was filled at a pump. The bucket had a dipper hanging on the side that was used for drinking by everyone. Bill and I would sleep on the porch that had big windows that were just 2x4's and screening. At night we would lower a big shutter that was held up by a rope. When the shutter was down it protected the screened area from the rain. The cabins had electricity but it came from Rosti's generator and when he went to bed, the generator was turned off.

Grandpa and Dad took Bill and me to Mission Lake once when Grandma and Mother didn't come along. Grandma helped with the planning, however, and we took everything we needed for our stay. Each meal was planned out in advance. We had no cooler but the trip only took 4 or

5 hours. I don't remember the things that we took but it did not include any pop, beer, potato chips, candy, or what we would call snacks today. We didn't have a radio or books either. This was a fishing trip.

We were driving through Anoka or Elk River when a policeman stopped us at a corner in town. He had been waiting for us and had a description of the car. He said Grandpa was to call home because of an emergency. Dad went with him to a place with a phone. We watched from the car. When they came back, we drove on in silence. One of us finally asked what had happened. We were told that we had forgotten the bacon. We were expected to go back for it but went on without it. Dad later said Grandpa was white with fear and some things were said about Grandma's judgement.

Driving to the lake was as much an experience as being there. We knew how far it was and how long it took. We kept track of each milestone as we passed it. One of the highlights each year was passing through the area around Lake Mille Lacs. The Indians would set up tepees along the side of highway 169 and sell baskets. It wasn't just one stand but many so we would say, "There is another one", as we drove by. We never bought any but it was quite a sight.

Cleaning fish was done in a small shed that was screened to keep the mosquitoes out. The shed was crude and had no water so we cleaned only the fish that we were going to eat. The bulk of fish were kept on ice in Rosti's icehouse and transported to Minneapolis in a big drum filled with crushed ice. The icehouse was an interesting place. The ice was covered with sawdust and we would put a gunnysack of fish on the ice under a layer of sawdust. We then tied a stringer around the top of the gunnysack and stuck it in the wall where we could find it again and keep it separate from other people's fish. Once when we were moving the sawdust we uncovered a big snake. We ran out the door but the door was on the second floor. Lucky for us we landed in a big heap of sawdust. We once saw a bigger snake and thought it was one of Rosti's that had escaped. We were told he had pet snakes. When gas rationing and tire shortages stopped others and us from going up there he closed the resort and went to Alaska. Many years later I drove through the Pine Shore Resort with my family and saw Rosti and talked awhile. He remembered our family.

During the war we went on vacation near home but always to a lake. One year we rented a cabin at Lake Washington from Clem Shoyer who was a contractor in town. I don't know how Dad knew him but he knew a lot of people. The lake had some undeveloped lakeshore in those days and Bill and I explored it. It was mostly in pastureland. Clem owned a good chunk of it and tried to sell some to my dad. We begged him to get it but he didn't think he could afford it. I think the spot was later sold to the Nordgrens. We caught two of the biggest bass I have ever seen the last night that we were there. Dad told us to go bobbing for bass near shore with a long cane pole and frogs for bait. For some reason there was a surplus of frogs along the shore and we had been shooting them with BB guns. We caught a few and went out in the boat at dusk. We would then plop the frogs near shore as though they had just jumped from the bank. We caught a nice bass and were coming in to show Dad how big it was when the second one took the line and pole almost out of the boat. We grabbed it just in time. We didn't weigh them but they were big.

Christmas

The first few Christmases that I recall were all the same. Mildred would dress up in a Santa Claus suit complete with a white beard that hung down too far and Bill and I were suppose to pretend it was Santa. She always looked and sounded like Mildred. She had such a whiny voice.

We didn't mind because there was always a clothesbasket

full of gifts that would appear. We would sit around in a circle and open the gifts one at a time. It was my grandparent's big show and sometimes Irv and Rufine were there with my folks. That was the entire family until Janice and Ann came along. After each opening there was the appropriate thank you to someone. This seemed like a strange twist if Santa had brought them. If we asked about that we were told 'so and so' ordered it from Santa. Grandpa always had a big tree and we were given some very nice toys. There was the fire chief's car with batteries for the head lights, the hook and ladder truck that sent the ladder up when it hit a wall, the two tractors that had treads like a tank, the cast iron fire truck, erector sets, the wind up train, and games like checkers and others with dice or cards. Of course, most of the boxes contained clothes like pajamas, wool stockings, mittens, and scarves. It was the one time each year that we caught up on the new sizes that we had grown into. I usually got the things that Bill grew out of but sometimes I would get a new one. If it was clothing, it was green for me and blue for Bill.

New Snowsuit

One of the best gifts was a new snowsuit that was a

two-piece. I had a one-piece red suit before that and was self-conscious about it because it was for babies. I dearly loved the new one.

There was an electric train at Grandpa's but it stayed there. Maybe it was given to Dad and Irv together when they were little.

One Christmas Bill and I got boxing gloves. I needed them like another hole in the head. There was no one my size and ability to box so I had to put up with others practicing on me. I think my grandparents got them with the feeling that no one could get hurt with those big gloves but they never got hit in the nose with them. We were taken to downtown Minneapolis to Dayton's at Christmas time to see the trains and figurines in their windows. There was plenty of music that made me feel more Christmas emotion. Music wasn't as easy to get then and we never got enough of it.

Traveling to Minneapolis doesn't sound like a big trip today because it was only 70 miles but in those days it was, especially if the weather was bad. In the winter we would find out about the road conditions by going over to the Greyhound bus terminal and asking if the buses were getting through. They ran quite often to Minneapolis and in all kinds of weather. We went to Minneapolis whenever the roads permitted but getting back home was a must no matter what. Dad had chains to put on the wheels when things got tough but that was a long trip in chains. It became even worse when a cross chain link came loose on one side and slammed the underside of a fender each time it came around. We went a long way like that once when Dad had no tool to reattach or dismantle the link.

We slid off the highway in our 1936 Ford on our way to Minneapolis one Christmas but no one was hurt. Dad said he had to turn toward the ditch to keep the car from turning over. A wrecker pulled us out of the deep snow and we continued on our way. When we got home from my grandparents' house we would have to check in by phone. Long distance rates were so high we would call person to person and ask for someone that wasn't there, like our dog. There was no charge for that.

Mother always wanted to have Christmas at home instead of at Grandma and Grandpa's so for a few years we had it both places.

Christmas in Mankato

Our tree was never as big but they were both real trees and smelled like pine. I missed the big production in Minneapolis. We would start by getting all the decorations out from last year like the paper-mache Santa Claus with his bag on his shoulder and one foot in the chimney. Decorating the tree was always fun, especially putting on the tinsel. It was made of tin foil strips that were saved from year to year so they were all matted together. We always started out putting them on carefully but always ended up throwing them at the tree. The lights were a problem because they were strung in series so when one light burned out, they all went out and you had to find the bad one by trial and error. Mother always put a sheet around the bottom to look like snow. After Ann was born, it was fun again for a few years because we started all over with the Santa Claus bit and Bill and I were warned not to spoil it for her. One year my cat would sit in the tree and look out at us.

Standard Oil CO used to have a Christmas party for the employees and their families that worked in the Standard Oil Office Building in Mankato. The bosses would appear on the stage in the proper pecking order and give out gifts to the kids. I can't remember what any of them were.

The anticipation of Christmas was always better than the event itself and there was always a let down afterwards. It seemed to be more fun to snoop at the packages under the tree and wonder what was in them. The countdown would start right after Thanksgiving and the paper would tell each night how many shopping days remained till Christmas.

When we got a little older we would draw names out of a hat and buy one present for someone outside of our immediate family. The adults would buy more practical things for each other like ties, handkerchiefs, cigarettes, perfume, and candy. When Grandmother was told to drink brandy to increase her circulation, everyone bought her a bottle. That was always fun because she was a teetotaler, except for what the doctor ordered.

Dad always had a dog. I remember him burying one in the back yard. It must have been Duke or Lady.

Bill, Clayt, and Duke

Lady wasn't with us long. Dad also had a dog that got so mean he had to find a farmer that would take him. The mean one was Jiggs (not to be confused with Uncle Irving's Jiggs) and Dad couldn't control him. I think he is the one that would go across the street and get into the chicken coop. Mother had to buy a few chickens that he got. She said she could see them flying up into the air. The final straw came when he wouldn't let Dad out of the car. It happened this way: Dad would park his car in the driveway in front of the house until it was time to put it away in the garage by the alley. He would then have to drive it half way around the block to the alley to put it away. Jiggs loved to go for rides so Dad would sometimes let him come along. One day Jiggs didn't think that was a long enough ride and wouldn't let Dad out of the passenger side of the car. For some reason, there wasn't enough room on the driver's side to get out. When Dad told us about this we asked, "What did you do?" and he replied, "I backed out and went around the block again." This time Jiggs let him out.

Mother, Dad and Jiggs

The Little Race Car

Dad built a little gasoline powered car for us that looked like a midget race car. He built it mostly for Bill because I was too young. Actually this was the second car he built. He made a push car before that. The push car wasn't very sophisticated. He used an old lawnmower handle to push it and if there were no one around to push it we would push it up a hill and coast down. That worked fine except once when Bill tried to stay on the sidewalk at the bottom of the hill, we turned over. No one was hurt.

Bill, Clayt, and the Car

The second car was actually a rebuild of the first one but it was a lot better. It was built on a steel frame and was powered by a gasoline washing machine engine. It even had a Model T steering column. The engine had a kick start lever and the magneto was wired through a knife switch on the dash so we could turn it off from the seat. It had only one speed (about 14 miles per hour). The motor was connected to the axle by a belt and two pulleys. There was slack in the belt until you pushed a pedal that was connected to an idler pulley that made the belt taught so the car would move. If your leg got tired, the car would stop. The tires were tubeless, air filled tires that were always going flat. They were just new on the market at that time. The car had an angle iron frame but there was no welding available so Dad had to hand drill holes in the steel and bolt things together. He worked on it in the basement during the winter and the garage during the summer. He and Grandpa joked about not being able to get it out of the basement. When the time came he had to take a lot of things back off in order to get it out the door. In the summer Dad would sweat so much drilling the holes that the water would drip off his nose. I wished I could sweat like that but I couldn't. The seats were upholstered and there was room for two with the steering wheel on one side.

When the car was just finished a neighbor kid asked how much for a ride and Dad told him 10 cents. He thought that would be the end of that but the kid came back with a dollar and said he would take 10 of them.

I'm not sure exactly when it was finished but we have moving pictures of it that my grandfather took in 1938. They were visiting on their way back from their California trip. The movies show Bill driving it around the yard with me riding. I was 5 years old that summer and Bill was 8. We thought that was plenty old enough to drive it in the street. As a matter of fact, Bill took me to school to get my kindergarten report card. We parked way out on the playground and I could see my teacher sitting on the school steps handing out the cards so I talked Bill into letting me drive it up to get my card. I'll bet that was a first for her. I had been allowed to drive it alone before but only on a racetrack that was at the fair grounds about a mile away. Bill would drive it over there following Dad's car.

The engine only held about a pint of gas so we had to carry a gallon can and a funnel up front by our feet. Sometimes we would pick raspberries in our backyard a sell them door to door for gas money. People were always surprised to see us come in the car.

Driving in the street became a problem, however, because the police would stop us and make Dad appear in court. Gus Johnson, my Dad's attorney, would get him off because the laws were not written to specifically handle a wash machine on wheels. It did force us to stay near home and sneak around the alleys and less busy streets.

Once when we were going down 4th Street, a dog gave chase. It was a particularly mean dog and I think his name was Sandy. We were told to avoid walking past his house whenever possible. Many dogs chased cars then and some even nipped at the tires. When we saw him start after us we were scared because we didn't have the protection of a regular car and he probably thought he finally found one his size. As we watched he reached full stride and ran smack dab, head-on into a tree. He yelped and fell in a heap. He never chased us again.

Dad was a pretty versatile person. He built a duck boat and trailer in addition to these two cars and all without power tools. If he had been a mechanic, it would have been no great surprise but he was an auditor with a degree from the University of Minnesota.

Standard Oil gave Dad a job and he was fiercely loyal to them. His job was always secure and that probably explains his loyalty. He did say, however, the first communication he got from the Company was a 10% pay cut that went to everyone. He put an emblem on the side of the little car that advertised their Iso-Vis oil. He sent a picture of it to the Standard Oil monthly magazine and it appeared in one of the issues.

The Iso-Vis Special

We were put out of business by the $20 war tax sticker that all cars had to have on the windshield. We didn't have a windshield or $20 and Gus didn't want to fight the Feds. The novelty was over by then and Bill was getting too big for it. Bill tried to make the front end longer but somehow it didn't work. It just sat on the back screen porch on Broad Street for a long time.

The house on Fourth Street was getting too small for our growing family, so the folks started looking for a larger one to rent.

Shortly before we moved someone threw a chain through the back bedroom window. It was where Ann was sleeping in a crib. My folks said it could have killed her had it landed in the crib. The police came and it was a very scary thing for all of us but we never found out who did it. My dad knew how to make enemies like the kid that ran over me in my bike or the Neuberts two doors away. I don't know how that feud started but Jerry would stand out in our sidewalk and shout obscenities at us. There were also bums around in those days. They usually stayed down by the railroad tracks and we would go down there to see them. They would come to the back door and beg for food but they didn't look that hungry and we thought they were just casing the place for something bigger. The chain incident probably had some impact on moving.

Part 2

The War Years

Moving

After first grade we moved across the alley to Broad Street. It would have been called 3rd Street but the street was extra wide and had a boulevard going down the middle. We even got a new telephone number. It became 2-9631 from 3-9201. We moved into the house where Al LaFrance had lived. Jim McKinney's family moved out of the one that the LaFrances bought which was across the street and up a few doors. We all moved the same day. We were still renting and the landlord lived next door. He was a crotchety old man by the name of Matt J. Graif. He owned a clothing store in town. I don't think he worked there anymore but it was still in his family. We lived next to the corner and he lived on the corner. We didn't have much of a back yard because Matt had his garden behind our house as well as behind his. He let us have a very small portion for our garden and clothesline.

When we couldn't find something, Mother would say it was lost in the move. We would argue with her and tell her we didn't leave any boxes at the old place nor on the truck so how could it be lost in the move?

1507 North Broad Street

Recent Photo of 1507 North Broad

The house was quite big and even had two bathrooms. We commented on how nice that would be when we would come back from a trip to Minneapolis and everyone had to go at the same time. There was one bedroom down stairs for Ann and we got to use it when we were sick. Ordinarily we slept upstairs where there were two bedrooms and a big bathroom. There was an entrance to an unfinished storeroom from the bathroom. Bill and I shared one bedroom and a bed that made it easier for him to push me out to peddle papers.

The furnace was still coal fired but it had a stoker that put the coal in automatically with an auger. For some reason we didn't get ashes but had to extract clinkers, which were about the size of a big sponge. Since they were still smoldering when we took them out to put them in a wash pail, the basement was always smoky. We also had a cistern for storing water that came off the roof. This water was soft and was used for washing. The city water was too hard for the soaps that were available. This house was quite old and the windows had to be held up with sticks. They weren't counterweighted like the windows in most houses. There was a porch across the front of the house and another one on the side in back. I had been on the back porch once before when Al LaFrance lived there and had a birthday party. We were bobbing for apples and I tried very hard to bite an apple but never got one.

We had some trouble with mice in this house and sometimes they would get pretty bold. There was one that came into the kitchen several times and raced around the table skidding on the linoleum all the way. He would then dive into a vertical cold air return. I wondered what would happen if I took the grate off and blocked the return with cardboard. We were watching when he came around the table and dived into the cardboard. He fell into a shoe that happened to be there. He got up, looked over the side of the shoe for a while as if to say, "What did you do?" Then he ran away. Mother was petrified at the sight of a mouse but she did agree that this one was kind of cute. I thought they were all cute with their long ears and beady black eyes.

When we left the house we would lock the front door with a big iron key which we then put into the mailbox. I think everyone did this, which seems strange because it was easy to get a skeleton key that would unlock all the doors in the neighborhood. The mailbox had a better use. . We used to get quite a bit of mail and most of it was first class. Letters were common between relatives and friends because it was the best way to communicate. Long distance telephone cost too much and trips were rare. The mailman would walk his route and come up each sidewalk to put the mail in the box. He carried all the mail in a big leather bag that was supported by a strap over one shoulder. People got to know the mailman like a friend.

Franklin School

Resent Photo of Franklin School

We went to a nice big school called Franklin School. It was built in 1928 and it is still a nice school today. It was kindergarten through 9th grade with the grade school separated from the junior high by a hill. The school was built on land that had a slope of about 10 feet per block so the playgrounds were on different levels. There were steps that led from one level to another. On either side, there were spillways to handle water. It was a fun place to go down on bikes; both the steps and the spillway.

We could watch the jr. high kids playing down on their playgrounds and wish we were that old. They even played tackle football (without any equipment, of course).

First, second, and third grades were pretty much the same thing to me. Each seemed to last forever and I couldn't wait to get to the next one. The seats were hard and

I didn't have much of a cushion. If everyone came to school we would get a star on a chart in front of the room. When we got so many stars we would get a 1/2 day off. That happened and it was wonderful. I even went one day when all the schools were closed for a snowstorm. It was the famous November 11, 1940, Armistice Day storm. I don't think I went until the next day, but it was still tough getting there. We had to go down the street between the drifts and kind of swim over the high parts.

School was pretty competitive and Joan Vosberg was the one to beat in arithmetic. We were given mimeographed sheets with addition, subtraction, multiplication, and division problems on them. We would race to see how many sheets we could do in the allotted time. I don't think anyone ever corrected them. Al LaFrance was good competition at other things and could spell Mississippi in 2nd grade. I wondered how he could do that. We cut up apples and dried them in the cloakroom. I was surprised at how sweet they tasted. I wore a Willkie button for President in 1940 and Al said, "A horse's tail is soft and silky, lift it up and you'll find Willkie." I went home and asked Dad for some ditty against Roosevelt but he could not come up with one.

I was taken to the principal in 2nd grade and she showed me the rubber hose. I don't think she ever used it but seeing it was pretty impressive. My teacher, Miss Hub, rescued me and chewed out the patrol boy who had taken me there for something innocently done.

The school didn't supply writing paper. Instead, we were told to buy 5 cent Big Chief tablets and give them to the teacher. When we needed paper, she would pass out the amount we needed. We had color crayons that we brought from home. There was only one row of them. I didn't know for years that there were bigger boxes with two or three rows in them. We had inkwells in our desks but we weren't allowed to have ink in them until 3rd grade. We looked forward to that time but when it came we found the pens were so awful we couldn't write with them worth a darn. The points would stick into the paper. Of course the paper was the rough cheap type that made it worse. The inkwells were usually half filled with spitballs anyway.

The teachers used to pick on Wayne Hoffman because he was left handed and preferred to write with his hand doubled back. This was not permitted and they made him wear a wire brace that prevented this.

Sometimes we would walk to the public library. It was quite a few blocks away. We went once when there was a puppet show. We were told how wonderful it was but I couldn't see much of interest in it. I liked the quiet there. I read a book about the three pigs and noticed that the print looked funny. There were long tails between the letters. It was hard to read at first but I finally realized that it was an introduction to 'script'. I was thrilled because now I would be able to read the letters between my folks and grandparents. The pig story was pretty good too. I think about it when a high wind blows down a house because houses are still made out of sticks.

In those days my nose ran all the time. I don't know whether it was from my dad's smoking or the dust in the house but my sleeves were a mess. Someone stole a nickel from someone else in 3rd grade and Miss Schmeising lined us up in the back of the room and started searching our pockets. She knew if she found a nickel, it would be the missing one. She reached into my back pocket and found a hanky that was put there because it was too used up to be in a front pocket. She gave up the search.

I liked to tell stories and exaggerate some things that had happened to my dad while hunting. Miss Schmeising knew some of the gals that worked at Standard Oil so the stories got back to him and from him to me. I learned it was a small world and I couldn't trust anyone. It was also the year the war began. I heard Roosevelt making the announcement on the radio. I didn't have any idea what it meant and things near me didn't change much for some time.

It was about this time when everything stated to get homogenized. Peanut butter used to separate in the jar with the oil coming to the top. It was a lot of work to stir it back in with a knife. Milk no longer had the cream on the top. This was not all good because cream was used separately in cooking and in coffee. The new homogenized mild was too rich with all that cream in it. The worst change came in the bread. I don't know if it was the homogenizing process that was used in bread but it no longer had holes of different sizes. This may sound trivial but the taste was affected too. It started to taste more like store bought bread instead of homemade bread. It was uninteresting.

We played marbles a lot on the school playground (there was no grass). When shooting marbles, the local rules prohibited hand motion to assist in the delivery of the marble. This was called fudging. If you were caught fudging someone would holler "no fudgees" and the shot would not count. Some marbles called "crocks" were not allowed as entry marbles because they weren't worth as much. I think they were made of clay. We all used a shooter that was a bigger marble and stood a better chance of making it back out the circle after it struck and ejected someone else's marble from the circle. Steel shooters appeared on the scene but were soon disallowed and were called "steelees."

Marbles were like money. You always knew how many you had and what they were worth in a trade. If someone ran out completely, there was a way to get back in the game. When the bell rang to start the day or to end a recess, someone would holler 'grabs.' That meant you could dive into a marble game circle and take any marbles you were strong enough to take. It wasn't pretty. I won Al LaFrance's last marble once and he had an awful time holding back his emotions. I felt so bad I wanted to give them back but I knew that would be an insult.

Once I was in the dime store and saw new marbles

for sale. I was shocked. I thought there were just so many in a neighborhood and they kept circulating. An outside supply could change their worth but I guess none of my friends ever got any that way.

Another favorite sport was jumping off the swings. It was hard to know when to jump. If you went too soon, you wouldn't get the distance (which was the goal) and if you waited too long, you would end up on your back. There was always talk about some big kid who got the swing to go over the top. We had a lot of brave souls try but it always ended in disaster. The merry go round was a waste of the school's money. We tried to get to go fast by climbing inside to push, but even at that there was no thrill.

In the winter we would play on the ice. There was always a place where the ice would accumulate so we could run to it and slide across. The fun came when everyone would do it at the same time so everyone would fall down at the far end in a heap of boys and girls.

May Basket Day was May 1 each year and it was a big day for young kids. We made May baskets in school out of colored construction paper. Our teachers were very careful to explain how it was done. First, we were to draw lines on the paper that were parallel to the edges and far enough from the edge so the we could see how deep the basket was going to be. The square in the middle showed the size of the bottom of the basket. Second, we were to use a scissors to cut along four of the lines but not any two that met. The teachers would hold a sheet of paper up and repeat the instructions several times before we began cutting. Then we would cut and always someone would cut a corner out and have to start over. We then folded the sides up and pasted the flap around the corner. Lastly we would paste a strip of paper across the top for the handle. We would take the baskets home and beg some goodies from our mothers to fill them. Usually popcorn was a major filler but there was fudge and other home made cookies or candies to put in. That evening we would go to a girl's house, hang the basket on her doorknob, and ring the doorbell. When the girl came we would run and she would chase with the intent on giving the boy a kiss. I put one on Nancy Lloyd's door once and she chased me and while I was running I thought it was dumb to run so hard but I did get away.

We used to send or give Valentines to each other but the schools got involved and had us make enough Valentines for everyone in the class. So we went through the process of getting one from everyone but we did put some special language in those that went to special people.

Across the street from the school there was a Coca-Cola bottling plant. We were allowed to go in and watch the bottles go down the line to get washed and filled. When they came to the end of the line, however, a man had to put them into cases. If we hung around long enough, the manager would give us a slug that would work in a machine to get a cold bottle of Coke. It was the only time we had any pop. No one had any at home.

In the other direction from school toward Front Street there was a small manufacturing plant that made machined parts for some war effort. We would find turnings in their scrap pile that we played with on the steps of the school. They could walk down the steps by themselves. Someone else knew this and patented it as the Slinky.

In 1986 and 1987 a classmate, Kathleen Lundin, and I put together a list of all the kids in our class that we could remember. It is as follows:

Students: Beverly Adams, Barbara Apple, Norma Apple, ---? Barnes, (kindergarten only), Duane Bengtson, Darlene Braun, Norman Buckmeier, Nancy Chandler, Stan Cooper, Barbara Cords, Janet Flitter, Wayne Hoffman, Francis Holcum, Jerome Kopp, Al LaFrance, Clayt Lagerquist, Nancy Lloyd, Kathleen Lundin, Jim Marinis, Lenore McVenus, Joe Mocol, Jon Nordgren, Karen Oversea, Don Peterson, Donna Puck, Ralph Rader, Jane Sargent,

Eudean Severens, Marilyn Sorheim, Myrn Swanson, David Sweigert, Lillian Swift, Don Tate, Ron Tilbury, Joan Vosberg. Joyce Wharton (4th and 5th) and Patsy Leitze are names added recently by friends but forgotten by me.

Teachers: Radcliff - Kindergarten; Winger or Poe(I had Winger) – First; Hubb – Second; Schmeising – Third; Chesser – Fourth; Scripture/Peterson – Fifth; Benson – Sixth(I had moved by then); Hawkins – Principal.

This list of students is too long to be one class. Some of these names are of kids that were with us at one time or another but not all the time. Some came and some moved away. Also, some were from the class ahead but joined us when they were held back for one reason or another. It was quite common to do this if you didn't keep up or were sick a lot. There were two first grade teachers but we had a grade and a half the other years. The class ahead of us was also big enough for a class and a half so we had one class with half 2nd graders and half 3rd graders. I was in one of these split classes when I was in the 2nd grade. It made it more interesting because you knew what to expect next year.

At a recent reunion, a picture of about half of our class was circulated. I'm not sure if it is 5th or 6th grade.

Classmates

Front Row: Francis Holcomb, Jon Nordgren,
        Nancy Lloyd, Janet Flitter,
        Lenore McVenus, Joyce Wharton,
        Darlene Braun, Patsy Leitze.
Second Row: Jane Sargent, Barbara Appel, --?
        Beverly Adams, ----?, Barbara
        Cords.
Third Row: Alice Chandler, Verle Stuve,
        Wayne Hoffman, Ralph Rader,
        Jerome Kopp, Don Tate, Stanley
        Cooper.
Back Row: Norma Appel, Kathleen Lundin,
        Everett Ewell (?sp), David
        Sweiger

In third grade I was already showing some of my non-cooperative side so I spent time in the hall for talking too much or being obnoxious. When Miss Schmeising asked why trees were green instead of brown I said, "They evidently don't like the color brown." I went to the hall where I thought I probably would never know the answer to that question.

My closest friends were Al LaFrance and Stanley Cooper. Stanley was the artist. He drew war scenes with trees and hills and clouds that looked like the real thing. Jon Nordgren was close behind but lived farther away. Karen Oversea was our favorite girl friend but she never showed any interest in any of us. I thought she was warming up once when she and her friends walked by our house and stopped to talk to me. I was sitting on the steps and they pointed at me and giggled. Finally one of them spoke. She said, "Your long underwear is showing." I guess that was a sin. Al LaFrance and I stopped at her house once to ask if she would go to the movies with us. She said, "No". We all walked to and from school in bunches that were dictated by where we lived. The girls in their bunch and the boys in ours. When we came out in the morning we would look for others and holler, "Wait up." Along the way we would find fun things to do like picking bees off of dandelions. This took some skill and you definitely had to get both wings. We would then put them on our belt so they would sting it. The stinger would stay in the belt as proof of how many you had gotten that day.

Rare Wartime Photo of Family, circa. 1942

Bicycles

Bikes were a big part of growing up. Since we had the run of the town, the bike provided the means to get around in it. My brother, Bill, got his first bike when he was 10 years old. It was a brand new black one. After much begging he taught me to ride it. I was told that when I was 10, I could have my own. I knew I couldn't wait that long.

I would have settled for a little one like Howie Schaub's. It wasn't much bigger than a trike but only had two wheels and didn't have a coaster brake. It was direct drive like a trike. His was the only one I ever saw.

Before I got my bike I was talking to Lillian Swift about bikes and she said she never used hers. I suggested that I buy hers for a few dollars and she agreed. I went home and got the money from someplace because everyone thought I was getting a good deal. When I went to her house to buy the bike, I told her mother about the deal and she shooed me away saying she knew nothing about it. I learned some things about Lillian and remembered not to take her seriously.

It wasn't too much later that I got my grandpa to buy me a real bike. He got it in Minneapolis from someone who put bikes together from junk parts. Mine looked like a kludged affair but I didn't care. It had parts from a Columbia and parts from a Silver King. Both were good bikes. It had an older Bendix coaster brake that was not as good as the Newdeparture like Bill's. Sometimes when I put the brakes on, the pedal went around backwards with no braking and sometimes it wouldn't catch going forward so it would just spin. The only parts I didn't like were the sprocket and the seat. The sprocket was so big around that I had to stand up to pump even when I was on level ground. This had the added disadvantage that when your foot slipped off the pedal, you landed on the bar with much discomfort. The seat was a big thing that looked like a tractor seat. It had a smooth leather top and huge exposed coil springs. I would love to have that seat today but then it wasn't stylish and I was very style conscious. Al LaFrance had an English bike with skinny tires. I was glad I didn't have that. It took years but I finally got a new seat for a birthday present. It was one of the best presents I ever got. Bill couldn't even keep the secret. He showed me where it was hidden.

Boys love to find out how mechanical things work so I soon took most of it apart. I soon learned how to fix flats and adjust the cones (wheel bearings). Bill took his Newdeparture brake apart and came close to not getting it back together since it was filled with washers that needed to be in the right order. My brake was easier to take apart and put together but all this looking never helped it's quirk of failing every once in a while. It also would break the little band that was attached to the frame. Of course, when that happened there were no brakes. It usually happened going down a hill. I took some nasty spills with that bike but never had to go to the doctor. We put leather bands on the axles that would polish the chrome whenever the wheel turned. Sometimes we used clothespins to hold cardboard in the spokes to make noise like a engine. We even learned to ride backwards by sitting on the handlebars and pedaling backward. Once one learned to balance this way, it was easy to ride except you couldn't see where you were going. I don't know how it got started or where they came from but squirrel tails were hung on radio antennas of cars and motorcycles. They soon appeared on bicycles as well hanging from the handlebars.

There was a bicycle patrol, called police boys, in town that was comprised of older kids that were given badges and police belts that went across their chests. I think Harold Beechied was one of them. They were the idea of some adult that thought he was doing a good deed. I don't know what they were suppose to prevent but when they went into action to arrest someone, it usually ended in a big fight. I was given a ticket once for leaving my bike in the street with a pedal on the curb. I went to 'court' in the police station on Saturday morning and was told that was dangerous because the bus came around the corner there. The 'judge' gave me a warning.

That old bike served me until I was 14 years old when I bought a new one with money I had saved. The new one was pretty special. I even bought a speedometer for it and spent a lot of time pedaling down hills to see how fast it would go. I used to ride it to work at the drug store. One summer night when it was completely dark I was taking my usual shortcut home and thought that I wouldn't have to go around the barn by the alley anymore because they had just torn it down. I was standing up pedaling when I ran into the foundation of the barn. It was about 3 feet high and made of limestone blocks. I flew through the air and landed softly in something but the bike had to be carried home. The fork was bent so badly that the front fender was smashed on the frame. I fixed it myself with great difficulty and sold it a short time later. All the years I rode bikes, especially when I was peddling papers, I wished the bike had an engine. There was one for sale called a Whizzer Motor Bike but they were way too expensive to even dream of having one. I think they were over $200.

Dick Ryan had a real fancy bike with all the extras including a knee-action fork. He was riding in the street one day and the whole front end collapsed. He fell headfirst to the pavement and put a small dent in his forehead from a small stone. I found out about this when I asked how he got the dent in his forehead.

Sunday School

My folks played an important role in molding my thoughts on right and wrong. They were not much for going to church but felt guilty when they didn't go. They sent us to Sunday school thinking that was the least they could do. For a while we went every Sunday with our little envelope with a nickel in it. It was kind of fun and all the other kids seemed to think it was all right, too. When I was in about 3rd grade they concentrated on telling all those stories about the flood, the whale, someone turning to a pillar of salt, and Adam and Eve. I told my mother I didn't believe that stuff and she said, "No one can make you believe anything. That has to come from within." Well, that was quite a relief and probably one of the best things she ever did for me. I was able to shake the guilt and went to Sunday school less often. Once when I went and hadn't been there for a long time, they put me in with the class ahead of mine. When I got confirmed it was with the kids that were in the class ahead of me in public school. I think it was Lin Barnes who talked me into going to confirmation classes. I became interested in church again during these classes and I asked a lot of questions. The minister told me I couldn't pick and choose the parts that I believed. I had to accept it all or none. I knew then, that this was not the church for me. If I wasn't allowed to think and ask questions there was no point in going so I didn't go much after I was confirmed.

Confirmation Class, circa.1946

Front row: Bob Hassing, Pat Bernhardson, --?--, Robert Farm, George Carlstrom, Harvey Brooks, Donna Dallman

Second row: Lowell Reedstrom, Clayt Lagerquist, Grace Nelson, Jack Bohan, Lin Barnes, --?--, Rev. Andreen

Third row: Gordon Holmgren, Harlow Norberg, Bob Nelson, Bob Ziemer, --?-

The Neighbors

The Peters lived next door. They were retired but I don't know from what. They didn't subscribe to the paper so I used to give them any extras I had. They didn't have a car so they walked to church each Sunday morning. They had a tradition in the way it was done. He would come out the front door and walk to the front sidewalk and turned left. At that moment she would emerge from the house and follow him at that distance all the way to church.

The LaFrances lived across the street. I played with the three older boys, who were Eugene, Albert, and Pierre. The family was a tight knit one and the three boys were almost always together. I liked to play with them but their mother preferred that they play together without me. She thought I was leading her boys astray. I wasn't always the one to lead them astray. I wasn't there when they were climbing over the fence to get in the pool area at Tourtellotte Park in the early spring one year. All was going well until Pierre lost his grip and fell back down. One of his hands was over the top of the fence at the time and he got hung up with the top of the fence buried in his wrist. The other brothers had to boost him up to get him off the fence.

They were Catholic and Democrat so it made for some interesting arguments.

Their grandfather came to visit from Wheeling, West Virginia. He was a very interesting man and liked to entertain us. He once blew smoke out of his eyes. Mr. LaFrance raised chickens in their back yard for a few years and it seemed out of character.

The Imms lived two doors away with the Peters' home in between. Val Imm was a state senator for many years and I distributed many of his re-election flyers. Their son, Bob, was my age but he went to a Lutheran school so we weren't the closest of friends. I did play in his sandbox quite a bit because it was the only one in the neighborhood. It was a nice one with a cover to keep the cats out and he had lots of toys and soldiers. We called them tin soldiers but I think they were lead. He had two older sisters and a younger one. Ruth and Valerie were the older ones and Trish was the younger one. I wonder if her name was Patricia. Valerie was the one that arranged so many of the neighborhood activities like the plays that were given in their garage. I had a part in them and she used to charge admission. I know Mr. Silber could always be counted on to be there. Valerie made up the entire play. One time I was suppose to come into the garage with a bow and arrow and say something and then make a hasty retreat. Everything went fine until I got to the door to leave. I had the bow crosswise to the door and it wouldn't go through. It took forever to get the bow vertical and the audience got a big bang out of it. I was accused of doing it on purpose just for the laughs but I hadn't.

I had my ups and downs with Mr. Imm. He didn't like me to steal his grapes that grew by the alley but he did let Bob and me sit on the front fenders of his Chevy and hang onto the headlights as he drove to the dump about a mile away. I peddled their paper but I had to go downtown to his weekly paper office to get paid. He always wrote a check against his paper for the Free Press. He was very conservative and so was most of Mankato so he was elected time after time. He is credited with getting money to expand Mankato State College while he was head of the Senate Finance Committee. He really turned nasty when I sold my paper route to someone other than Bob. Maybe he also knew we didn't hand out all his flyers. Many of the flyers would find their way to the storm sewers. Mrs. Imm almost ran over Ann when she was a toddler. I don't remember this but my mother told us many times that Mr. Peters saved her. Ann was sitting on Imm's driveway when Mrs. Imm was backing out of the garage. Mr. Peters called to Ann to come to him and she did. I guess there wouldn't have been time to do anything else.

The Imm's also had a young son named John. He locked himself in an upstairs bathroom and my dad had to climb a ladder and go in the window to get him.

I was always interested in girls even though I was afraid of the ones I really liked. It is easy to fall in love with someone that looked like Amy Lou Krick. She had black hair that was parted down the middle with two pigtails hanging down in back. She had a pretty face but it is hard to describe it other than to say it was just right. She was older than I and maybe my brother's age. As a matter of fact he may have admired her and called her to my attention. She took music lessons from Mrs. Silber, like so many others, and would appear at the same time each week. She rode her bike and parked it against a tree in the park (boulevard). I was usually nearby on my bike and would be able to say something in passing. I think she knew I was Bill's brother and was polite.

I was content to admire her from a distance. She had an older sister, Donna, who would baby-sit Ann occasionally. She was there once when I came home from school. I showed her a drawing of a swan that I had done in school and she made such a thing of it I thought it must be good. They moved away shortly after that and I never heard of her again.

Helping Mother

Sometimes I would help mother with the laundry and I thought it was fun. There were times when she didn't want to go down to the basement because it made her rheumatism flare up. We had a wringer wash machine and the two wash tubs. When I ran the laundry from the wash water through the wringer to the rinse tubs I would play games. I would fill up a sock with water before putting it in the wringer so I could watch the water spray out of it when it hit the wringer. Pillowcases were even better but if you weren't careful they would touch the sides of the wringer and get grease on them. We would hang the clothes up outside whenever possible, even in the winter. When they froze, I couldn't figure how they could dry. They couldn't be out too long in the winter because the soot from the coal furnaces would get them dirty again just like it did to the snow. In the summer it was easy and they smelled so good.

The socks were put over the line and held by a clothespin. This sounds all right but when they came down, they still had that bend in them. Before they could be put away, someone had to run a hand in them and make them round again. The socks always had holes in the back and I learned how to darn them but the fix didn't last long.

Occasionally I was sent to the store to buy some groceries but most of the time they were delivered. Mother would telephone the store and talk to the grocer about the things she wanted and to find out if they were fresh that day. She would place her order and charge it. The groceries were delivered by a delivery boy who had a collapsible wooden box. At the end of the month Dad would give Mother some money but never enough to pay up the bill at the store. There was also a store on fourth street. I think it was called Tillman's then. They used to sell comic books there but I never wanted to spend a dime on them. Some kids would put one inside another and get two for the price of one. There was usually a poker game going on in the back room so it seemed like an interesting place. It was just down the street from the mean dog, Sandy, so I didn't like to go there.

Every once in awhile we would change stores and drive across town to get the groceries cheaper but it always ended up the same, we couldn't pay up at the end of the month. Mocol's store was nearby and run much like a modern supermarket but I think they dealt only in cash so we didn't go there very often. Sometimes we would drive to a butcher shop on Front Street to get meat. If Bill and I were along, the butcher would come out to the car and give us a cold wiener. I guess that was suppose to be a treat. We would ask Mother to buy his 'chicken wings' because they were our favorite. Actually they were bits of pork and beef put on a wooden stick. Mother fried them in the black iron frying pan and they were really good.

Washing and drying dishes was a chore for a family of five. Bill and I used to take turns drying for two or three minutes each until the job was done. We both hated it with a passion. I used to dream about an automatic machine that would do this for us. I pictured a table with all the plates and silverware held in place while they turned upside down and were washed from below. That way both the washing and setting were done by machine. Dreaming didn't help.

Tonsillectomy

When I got sick I was taken to the Mankato Clinic. The whole building smelled like alcohol. They tried many times to figure why my nose ran all the time but nothing worked. Finally they took out my tonsils because my colds always went to my throat. I was given ether and it felt like I was drowning up side down. I was carried to the car and driven home at the end of the day by my dad and put in the downstairs bedroom. He said the whole room smelled like ether and wondered if they had given me too much. The next few days I was given a lot of ice cream. It didn't make it worth it but it helped.

Peddling Papers

When Bill was 10 years old he got a paper route. You had to be at least 10 to get one. He soon taught me to peddle his route so I could be his substitute. It was a Minneapolis Tribune route and had only about 19 daily papers because most people took the Mankato Free Press on a daily basis. The bad news was that it was spread out over a mile and the papers weren't delivered to your route. They had to be picked up at the Tribune Office that was another 6 or so blocks away from the first customer. Here a 'boss' would count out the papers and take your money once a week.

Sunday was especially interesting because the Free Press didn't publish a paper so every one wanted the

Tribune. This meant a route of this size had about 100 Sunday papers and they were big even then. Bill taught me the Sunday route also, which meant getting up at about 4:00AM so the papers could be out by 6:00AM. I hated getting up early, especially in the winter. We had to dress in a cold house and go outside where it was worse. If it was really cold we would put on two pairs of pants. Once I was up and outside, it was very nice. No one else was out and it was like you had the whole town to yourself. In the winter the sulfur smell from the coal furnaces reminded me of a cozy warm house. In the summer the birds would seem tame and flocks would strut in the street at the intersections.

It wasn't too much later that Bill got a second route and I peddled his old one. He was still in charge and went with me to collect. The Sunday alone was 15 cents and a lot of people put the money out on their porches so we didn't have to go there to collect. Even with this help, there still was a lot of time spent at night getting the rest of the money each week. We walked around town at night with a big sack of money and never worried about something happening to it. When we went to collect, we would be invited to stand inside the front door while someone went to get the money. Every house smelled differently and I wondered how many I could have identified had I been blindfolded. When we weren't peddling or collecting we were out looking for new starts. The paper office always had some prize for the carrier that came up with the most new starts during some time period. Sometimes we would get a bingo card for each new start and we would play bingo for prizes at the paper office.

If I got through peddling and had a paper left over, Bill would go through each customer with me and ask if I had peddled that one. I would remember which one it was occasionally but most of the time a call would come to the house that someone didn't get their paper. I wasn't too concerned about that but Bill would have a fit. Couldn't I ever learn to do it right the first time? My mind was some where else most of the time and I peddled without thinking about it. I got a new start on Vine Street and peddled it for a week but when I went to collect, they said they didn't order any paper. When I told the boss, he drove me there to speak with them. When we got there I said, "No, not this house; it's the one down there a couple of blocks." He said, "No that's Lime Street; this is Vine Street." The street signs looked the same to me like push and pull today.

One Sunday Bill had agreed to take Cobby Klagas's route because he was on vacation or something. That meant we had over 300 papers to deliver. We got up at 2:30 and met the truck from Minneapolis at the office. We took a wagon and a cart that attached to a bicycle and filled a couple of bags that were put over the bikes and we started. It started to rain and looked hopeless. Bill found a phone and called Dad and asked if he would bring the car. Dad said, "You got yourself into this, you get yourself out." I have wondered about this ever since. Would I have done this to my kids? Did we get the papers delivered? Yes, we had no choice. We peddled the first one and then the second one. We got done but not on time and the papers weren't all dry.

This was only the beginning of my paper carrying days. I had a route continuously from then until I was 14. The routes got better, however, and finally I got an afternoon Free Press route. It had close to a 100 daily papers and most were within a 4 or 5 square block area. The last 7, however, were on top of the Good Counsel Academy hill. This was a Catholic boarding school for girls and nuns in training. The Priest got one paper at his residence, one went in a box attached to the corn crib (for the farmer), one went to the laundry, one went to the person who lived next to the laundry, two went to the main school building and I can't remember where the other one went. Delivering the paper to the farmer was easy but collecting was something else. It wasn't that he didn't pay, but it involved going back to the farm house which was some distance, then help him count out the change each month from his supply of pennies and nickels in a big jar. He was nearly blind, at least for close up vision, so he had to examine each coin for some time before he would know what it was. His wife was there but offered little help. They were such nice folks and enjoyed talking to me, or anyone else that came, so it took an awfully long time to collect.

I used to enjoy this place once I got up the hill. Sometimes I would carry my bike up the front steps and count them. There were over 200. Usually I would push the bike up the back road. In the winter I walked. The nuns at the school would give me candy at Christmas and sometimes the girls would open a window and talk to me. The laundry was a particularly depressing place because those young nuns would have to work so hard ironing all those outfits. I usually finished at about 6:00PM and would go straight home. Sometimes in the summer I would get done early and dilly dally around the place. They had their own apple orchard and water tower. I enjoyed climbing their water tower so I could look out at the whole valley. Once I sat up there and smoked a cigarette. I got a little dizzy and figured that wasn't such a good idea.

My next route was better because it didn't have the Good Counsel Academy hill but I did have to go up to the top of the hill south of there for 2 papers. Since Mankato was in a valley cut by the ancient rivers, all the hills were the same height but it was easier to get up this one. One of the two customer on this hill was Dr. Kearny and he had built a stairs and ramp from Madison Avenue above 6th Street so it was only about half as high from there. One really cold day I had both of my hands in the paper bag between the papers so they would stay warm. I tripped on a step and landed on my nose. I got an extra bump on my nose that lasted for years. The other customer up there was Mrs. Kimble and I used to bring her mail up from 6th Street.

I was walking my route one day along 5th Street and wondered about my memory. How long could I remember some incidental happening? I shut my eyes for a moment and then gave a quick glance up toward 6th Street. I tried to remember what I had seen like a picture. I made note of the houses on the left and the lack of them on the right. A car was going across 6th Street. I thought of that picture several more times that day and again other days. I can still see that picture.

I used to notice all the houses that had stars in their windows representing a son or a daughter in the service. I thought this is such a proud time. One house had 5 stars sewn on their plaque. One day I noticed that a red star had been replaced with a gold one that meant that one had been killed in action. I felt so bad I was afraid to go there to collect because I didn't know what to say. I think their name was Morrison.

I think each of these routes belonged to Bill before I got them. I kept this route for a long time after we moved to North Mankato even though it meant an extra mile or two from home. In the winter I used to take the short cut across the frozen river. This was tricky, however, because there was always open water that had to be avoided and it moved from day to day. I used to stop in Mocol's store on the way home and if I had an extra paper (and I usually did) I would read the war news to Honna Mocol. He was from Syria and couldn't read English but wanted to keep track of the war effort. He ran the vegetable department and would pay me for the paper and then tell me I could sell it again to someone else, which never happened. It did give me a chance to hang around the store and steal cigarettes.

I still had this route when the atomic bomb was dropped on Japan. The other paperboys on our corner asked me what an atomic bomb was so I told them. I was wrong, of course, but I felt I was expected to know everything.

I finally got a route in North Mankato. It was great except for a couple of people that wouldn't pay me. There were 4 or 5 routes that got their papers delivered to the municipal building. We would fold all the papers before we started. I would put the bag on my bicycle basket and toss the papers into the front yards. I could do the whole route in about an hour. One summer there was such a polio scare that the paper bundles were dropped a block apart because no one was allowed to assemble in groups.

The paper cost 80 cents a month and I used to make about $20. Dad said he wished he had $20 a month to spend like I did. I don't know where all the money went but I did buy all my own clothes and for a while I paid room and board of $2 a week. I kept this route until my 14th birthday when I got a job in the drugstore.

Caddying

On Broad Street, I lived close enough to the Mankato Golf Club to be able to get there on my bike and learn to caddy. Again, it was Bill who did it first and prepared me to start. Once you were caddying in a 4-some you got lots of help from the other three caddies. It was always like this. The older kids taught the younger ones. It wasn't like you might think, however. Criticism was ever present, compliments were non-existent. There were always more caddies hanging around the Caddy Shack than were needed and the Pro, Mac, decided who was to caddy for whom. I got to shag balls before I got to carry a bag. Shagging was fun. There was no driving range at the course so when Mac would give lessons, someone had to get the balls back. You didn't wait until all the balls were hit, however, you chased after each ball after it was hit.

My first big chance came when I was given the bag of a pretty good golfer. It turned out he was a pretty good guy, as well, because he could tell it was my first assignment and he patiently told me how to do everything starting with how to present the bag to him for his club selection. Mostly, we were there to carry the bag and find the ball. If your guy or gal was first on the green, you held the pin and pulled it at the right time. Other than that we were to keep quiet.

We got paid 50 cents for 9 holes and 75 cents for 18 holes. It interfered with peddling papers so I had to get a 'job' in the morning or anytime on Sunday.

Often times a trip to the Golf Course was for naught because more senior caddies got all the jobs. As we hung around the Caddy Shack, we would play a tiny course that had been hacked out by the caddies. No full swings, just chips. Saturday mornings the caddies were allowed to play the 9 hole course if we could get started shortly after dawn.

I caddied for women quite often. Maybe the senior caddies didn't come on ladies' day. Sometimes they were so short of caddies I got to carry two bags. For some reason I caddied for the same two women so often I got sick of the expression, "Nice one, Madge." Margaret Stratman was married to a lawyer in our neighborhood and hit the ball the same every time and every time it was, "Nice one, Madge." These two were talking about sex one time and one of them warned the other that I could hear. The other one said, "So what, he doesn't know what we are talking about anyway." Maybe I didn't, but I still got a bang out their talk because one of them thought it would be nice to invent a kind of a sling so he wouldn't squash her so much.

We went looking for lost balls when it was apparent that no jobs were forthcoming. When members bought golf balls from the Pro, he put their names on them with a device that imprinted their name with indelible ink. If we found one of these we would get 5 cents from the Pro if we turned it in to him. Usually we took them home and removed the name with nail polish remover and sold them for more than 5 cents to someone who would overlook the indentations.

While I was caddying, I bought some used clubs that lasted quite a while but when I moved to North Mankato I was too far away from the Golf Course to go very often.

Mowing Lawns

Some of our neighbors paid someone to mow their lawns. I was envious of my friends who got these jobs even though it was hard work. There weren't any power lawn mowers so they had to be pushed. My Dad always had his blades adjusted tight so the cut was clean but this made it hard to push. I got a job cutting the lawn at the store across the street one time but left our mower there when I got done. Dad asked where it was and I told him. I stayed out of his way for quite a while.

Union School

In the summer after third grade, the High School burned down. This changed everything. Lincoln Junior High was used as a High School so the junior high kids were bused to Franklin and our fourth, fifth, and sixth graders were bused to Union School where they were crowded in with the 'special' kids that were already there. Two buses were used to take us the six blocks or so to the other school but hardly anyone got a seat. Most of us would be standing in the aisle so it was filled all the way to the door.

A Recent Photo of Union School

Going to Union School for 4th and 5th grades represented quite a change. Life didn't seem quite so innocent. World war II was on and it wasn't going well. The mood sort of rubbed off on everything else. Talk at school was about the war and it's heroes and it seemed to us that we were being cheated out of all that glory because we were too young. We all had recruiting pictures on our bedroom walls. Mine were all Navy related. We bought war stamps at school for 10 cents and put them in a stamp book that totaled $18.75 when full. At that time (I don't remember it ever happening) we could trade it in for a bond that would be worth $25 in ten years. We also learned to knit so we could make little 6 inch squares out of wool that eventually were sewn together to make blankets for the soldiers. I think Kathleen Lundin's mother did the sewing. Vacations were canceled for lack of gas and tires. I used to walk home for lunch and Dad would usually give me a ride because he came by at that time for his lunch. When he started car pooling with Mr. Joe Meyer, he was afraid to ask him to stop for me because he said it took too much gas to start and stop. Rationing was not only on gas; sugar and meat were also rationed and required ration coupons. I stole meat coupons from my mother to buy meat for my cat. I had the money from one of my many jobs but had no way of getting ration coupons. Toothpaste tubes must have been made of tin because we had to turn in an old one to buy a new one. Scrap iron drives were common and people gave everything they could. I still remember my brass bed out in front leaning against the tree waiting to be picked up. I wonder who benefited from that.

There was not much time to play on the school grounds because the bus would get us there just in time to go in. Playing on the school ground had resorted to roughhousing. Don Johnson got caught throwing me over his shoulder. The principal just happened to be walking past and took us to her office. She soon let me go but there was a scuffle between Don and the principal and as a result, he was sent to a boy's school. We no longer played marbles and the girls were less sociable. We didn't mingle with the 'special' kids at Union but you could tell which ones they were because their pants were always too short.

I wore knickers and had boots with a knife pouch. Our pants had no zippers so it was imperative to keep as many buttons as possible. If you had all your buttons on the fly some friend would grab and pull so you were no better off than the others. We always had a knife with us and the boots were often in need of repair. The half soles would come loose and when I walked I would have to kick that foot forward to get the sole to flop into place before I could step down on it. It wasn't hard but sounded funny because it would go flop flop flop. I could get them re-stitched for a dime at the shoemaker that lived on the way to school. He had a shop in the front porch of his house.

We carried lunch pails and drank milk that cost 1 cent for a half-pint. It was delivered to the school every morning from some government program that was designed to make sure the poor people at least got some milk to drink. I shouldn't make fun of this because there were some pretty poor kids in our class especially some from the 'prairie.' Mother bought cookies from a kid in our class once and I asked her why she did that. She said, "Evidently they need the cash now worse than we do." We didn't have much money but Dad always had a decent job. Once my mother didn't make a lunch for me but gave me money to 'eat out.' There were no fast food places then so I went to the Blue Blazer for lunch. It was a nice dining room in the Saulpaugh Hotel. When my dad found out, he couldn't believe it. I guess that place was too spendy for him.

I had Miss Chesser for a teacher in fourth grade and she used to eat the chalk. She also enjoyed embarrassing us. If she had something on us she would make us stand in front of the class while she asked us questions about it. That was the year Jane Sergeant tried to steal a box of watercolor paints. She hid it in her overshoe. When the count of boxes came up one short a massive search was underway but came up with nothing. Not until we lined up to go home did the clop clop of her overshoe yield the paint box.

A highlight of these years was getting a trombone. Mr. Hesla had been hired by the school system to teach instruments to the grade school kids. I wanted a trombone and we got a rent-to-buy one at a local music store. It was beautiful and smelled like metal. For a long time it seemed I was told to practice only with the mouthpiece but finally I started playing. My grandparents gave me a music stand (which I still have) and sometimes my dad would play the accordion with me.

Miss Scripture was one of the best-liked teachers. She taught 5th grade and drove a model T. She started out the year but something happened and we got a different teacher. I guess I didn't like her replacement much because

I couldn't even remember her name. Kathleen Lundin supplied it later. Her name was Peterson and she was the one that took me to the Principal when I got caught smoking. Miss Scripture even took us on a picnic before school started or shortly thereafter. We were told to bring a lunch and a raw egg and some newspaper. We met at the sand caves across the river from Sibley Park. We built a fire and soaked the newspaper in river water. Then we wrapped the eggs in layers of paper until they got as big as a baseball. Next we put them in the coals from the fire. We each had a hardboiled egg.

My Free Time Activities

The games we played away from school changed as well. In the winter we went to the ice skating rink most nights. The city had flooded an empty lot near the school and built a warming house with a coal stove in it. A really nice guy from the city would tend the fire and flood the rink during the day. I didn't spend much time on the ice because my skates were so big I couldn't keep from skating on the outsides of them and this made my feet ache. This pair was my mother's and we put newspaper in the toes. I never had a new pair of skates but I did get some that fit better than hers. Once in a while there would be a sleet storm and cover the roads with ice. We would put on our skates and skate all around the neighborhood. When the conditions were just right, we would hang on the back bumper of the bus and 'ski' with our overshoes down the street. The bus stopped as it got to Broad Street so we would get on there and go up a couple of blocks, then over to Fourth Street and back to within one block of home.

When we went skiing it was an all day affair. The snow conditions had to be just right. Wind blown crust made it hard to get to the hill let alone ski down it. Warm days made for sticky snow and bitter cold days made it no fun. I never went alone so someone else had to be in the mood. Just getting ready was a chore. It started with long underwear. Shirt, pants, and a sweater came next. Then came the shoes with long socks over the shoes and pant legs followed by another pair of pants. Usually the second pair of pants was the same size and type as the first pair so they were hard to put on. The jacket was next, followed by the overshoes, scarf, cap, and mittens. Walking with all these clothes was hard and we were a long way from the Good Counsel Academy, hill where we usually went.

Aunt Rufine would hand knit long wool stockings in the shape of a tube without a heel so they would fit anyone and could be used over shoes. We always wore a scarf. It could be used just around the neck but also across the face when it was really cold. Our breath would cause icicles to form on the outside of the scarf. First we had to walk to the hill, then go over a barbed wire fence, and cross the creek before we could put on the skis and 'cross country ski' across the pasture to the hill. If we were lucky, others were there before us to pack a trail. If not, we would side step up the hill with our skis packing it as we went. We went to the top of the hill in an area that was ideal. I think it was an old road up the hill so it made it a gradual slope but the last 50 feet or so we would leave the old road and go up the steep part where there were no trees. If we could get down the first part without falling we could usually go all the way to the bottom. Once I couldn't stop at the bottom and went crashing into the creek. I thought my ankle was broken because the tip of the ski was pointed in the wrong direction but it turned out that only the ski was broken. I tried to repair it with a tin can and nails but it never was as good after that.

Going home was just as difficult as getting there because we usually stayed too long and got too tired. Getting these clothes off again was even more of an adventure because we were cold and wet. The snow would pack in between the two pair of pants and come off in the house. Everything had to be hung up on a line to dry so we usually got help from Mother.

In the summer we played lots of games. When we played baseball, the trick was rounding up the right kids so we would have the equipment. When we were short of players we played 2-a-cat. If you got to first base you got a free pass to third base. We had a fielder's glove and would lend it to the other team when we were up to bat. I was running the bases once and someone threw the ball toward the base but hit me on the head. I woke up on the sidelines. No one was concerned once they got me off the field.

We played some basketball as well. There was a hoop on the old garage behind our house by the alley. I call it the old garage but it probably wasn't any older than the house but it looked like a shed. We acquired a basketball somewhere so we played 'horse' with anyone around. The basketball didn't hold air very well but we had a tire pump and a needle. We also had a football that we bought new. It was one of Dad's weak moments and I think our grandparents were visiting. He gave us the money and told us to go to Mahowald's and buy a football. This was the only store around that had sporting goods. Bill and I walked there and bought a junior size ball. It was a great ball for many years. It took a beating when it landed in the street so sometimes we just kicked it across the street onto the boulevard.

Since Mocol's grocery store was across Broad Street from Franklin School, we went into the store quite often even when we went to Union School. Grandma Mocol had her own little corner in the store where she sold candy. We didn't often have money to buy candy but in 1942 the government started minting zinc pennies. The looked a lot like dimes to Grandma Mocol and we often tried to get two nickel candy bars with one. She was wise to us but if we insisted she would sometimes give in and give us the candy. Joe Mocol was in our class and knew about our ploy but he said it didn't make any difference because Grandma didn't put much money into her till anyway. She used to ring up the sale but put the money in her pocket. At the end of the day she would take the money upstairs and put it in a sock.

When we didn't have an organized game to play we went for walks and sometimes went way out of town and took a lunch along. It was fun to go out Thompson road by the Good Counsel Academy. This ravine followed the creek that came through town. As the creek went east out of town it cut a swath through some little hills that made banks about 6 feet high. The swallows made holes in these banks for their nests. If I approached from the top I could put my hand over a hole and try to catch a swallow as it came out. I tried several times but the guy that lived across the street would holler at me to leave them alone. There were farms out there and once we played for hours on a haystack. We could climb to the top and jump or dive off. I dived once and bent my neck back so bad that I saw stars. The farmer saw what we were doing to his stack and chased us away. I found out later the LaFrance boys were caught and their dad had to take them out there to apologize. We didn't know that if the haystack wasn't made just right, the rain would get in and spoil the hay.

Our neighborhood games included war games with rubber guns. We were first introduced to them by Grandpa when he made rifles for Bill and me. The guns were made of wood and they shot rubber bands that were made from tire inner tubes. They were cut into strips like rubber bands with knots tied in the middle. The pre-war rubber was much better than the artificial rubber and could be stretched to great lengths. One end of the band was put on the end of the rifle and the other was held in a clamp made from a spring-loaded clothespin. The clothespins weren't strong enough by themselves but we would add layers of rubber bands to re-enforce them. When they were fired all we had to do was squeeze the clothespin at the bottom and it would release the rubber band. They were intended for target practice but we soon found them to be good for our war games. We would carry several including a pistol sized one. If you hit someone in a war game they would have to count to 500 out loud before they were allowed to fight again.

We never got into trouble with the police but it was fun to toy with them. The big kids in the neighborhood would somehow notify the police that kids in our neighborhood were shooting windows out with BB guns. The police would come and the kids would stand around with BB guns until they were seen by the police, then they would run. Some of the kids would even put a gun down a pant leg and go to the police car to talk to them. I didn't carry my gun but I thought it was exciting to be there and be visible.

We played on the pastures surrounding Good Counsel Academy. We played baseball there using dried cow pies as bases. It is also where the bigger kids would shoot arrows up in the air to see how high they would go. No one worried about where they might come down as long as they were found. For a while there was an effort to catch gophers and turn in the legs for a 25 cent bounty. Some kids would pour water down their holes and snare them when they came up for air.

The store across the street was the same one I went to from 4th Street but now it was close enough to hang around when nothing else was happening. It was just a small grocery store but they did sell other things that kids liked. There was always some promotional item that we all had to have. Little balsa wood sailplanes were popular off and on. Yo-yos were big once but the one I liked best was a propeller that could be spun with the pull of a string. The string was wound around a spool on a dowel. The spool was attached to the propeller only when it was not spinning. It would lift off the spool and go higher than the trees. If you were lucky it wouldn't stay up in one. They also had punchboards there because gambling was legal then. I won 12 jawbreakers on a penny punchboard once, but that was the only thing I ever won.

I loved to go to the Mankato Airport. I often times rode my bike but it was up on the hill and sometimes it meant pushing the bike. There were always meadowlarks out near the airport and I used to look forward to hearing them sing. They often perched on the telephone lines along the dirt road. I went alone usually and just hung around the hangers and talked to whoever was there. The hangers had a special smell of airplanes and there were always birds in the rafters. The echoes of the high metal roof amplified their voices. The airport wasn't very busy and the planes mostly sat in the hangers. I got to know a couple of the mechanics and after a while they let me help them. They would let me wash and wax airplanes all day for a 15 minute ride in an airplane. I thought that was wonderful. After a few tame rides they would do some wingovers and stalls that brought my stomach to my throat. They even had access to a Stearman and took me up in that -- open cockpit and all. I told Bill about the airport deal I had so he came along and got a ride with me in the Stearman.

Dad liked airplanes, too, and once drove us up to see a Ford Trimotor that was scheduled to come in. We got to see it for a long time because it got stuck in the mud.

Bill and I spent a lot of time building model airplanes when we were in grade school. They came in kits that were priced from 5 cents. They contained everything you needed including the glue. The 5 cent ones were pretty small and sometimes scrimped on the glue or paper but we made a few so we could set them on fire and sail them out the window. The dime models were much better but usually ended up the same way. We would build one and fly it until it was destroyed before we started another one. They were powered by a rubber band that was wound up with the propeller. We would sail them first to get the nose weighted just right. The 25 cent models were big and pretty and could be used to admire for a while. We especially liked the warplanes, like the Spitfire and P40. Finding places in the house to work on them was a chore because each one required a dedicated table. Later on we built a couple of sailplanes with 5 feet wingspans but never got them to go way up in the air. I even got interested in making models again in high school and built a place under the basement stairs that was dedicated to them.

We went to the movies quite often because we had money from the paper routes. It cost 12 cents with 10 cents for the movie and 2 cents for the war tax. There were three theaters in town and each had two different movies per week. They were called The State Theater, The Grand Theater, and The Time Theater. There was usually only one good movie showing at a time and standing in line to get in was a routine event. Some of my friends would see the same movie twice. I couldn't figure out why they would do that because I could remember the whole thing the first time. If you didn't get there early enough, you had to sit down in the front rows and look up at the screen. There were ushers with flashlights that tried to keep order but there was always some wisecracking going on. In the lobby we could buy candy and popcorn. My favorite candy was the dark Walnettos. The main feature film took only part of the time. The rest of the time was showing cartoons, shorts, and news. It was a good place to catch up on the war news from a documentary called the *March of Time*. It showed lots of battle footage with maps and commentary. It wasn't full of propaganda the way many of the feature films were, but sometimes they stopped the movie at this point and passed a plate for donations, presumably for the war effort. Many of the movies were full of war propaganda (which wasn't considered a bad thing). They had close-ups of the 'dirty Japs' and 'German krauts' that made anyone hate them. Their airmen would shoot our men while they were coming to the ground in a parachute after bailing out.

The shorts were not very good and sometimes had unknown comedians doing skits. Even the well-known ones, like the Three Stooges weren't very funny to me. I liked the cartoons best especially the Walt Disney ones with Bugs

Bunny, Mr. Magoo, Tweety Bird, and The Road Runner. They all ended with Mel Blank's voice of Porky Pig stuttering, "That's all, folks."

If the movie were a good western, we would walk home by the alleys so we could pretend to shoot each other from behind garages and telephone poles. We made all the noises of the guns and ricocheting bullets with our mouths. On Saturday mornings there was a free movie if you could get enough Wonder Bread wrappers. We couldn't eat that much bread but we had friends without kids that would save them for us. One Saturday, Bill had a good idea. We didn't have enough wrappers so he simply cut a few in half. Who would know? He got caught and I went to the movie without him. The movies were not first run movies but sort of a serial of second class westerns. They would end with the hero tied to a railroad track with the train coming. The next week there was some sort of a miraculous escape and the show would go on.

We had a cork gun or at least that's what it was called. There were no corks with it. I asked about this several times but got no answer. It was made like a small double-barreled shot gun and would cock when it was bent in half. This cocking action would pull a shaft against a spring to a stop position. When the triggers were pulled it would release the shafts as if to propel a cork. It made a bang and we were content to use it this way. I assume it came with corks but my folks figured that it would be too much of a good thing to have corks flying around the house. We also had pistols that shot darts with rubber suction cup ends. They would stick to smooth surfaces like the target or a window. They also were spring loaded and were cocked by pushing the darts into the barrel until they came to the stop. They disappeared after they were used only a short time.

Finally we got BB guns. A BB gun was a wonderful thing for a kid. I carried mine everywhere. It fit across the handlebars of my bike where I could hang on to it without noticing that it was there. I shot at all sorts of things and soon learned to see the BB come out of the end of the barrel. It was surprising to see how fast it would drop from the original trajectory. With this knowledge I could aim above things and have a better chance of hitting them. Glass was a good target because it would shatter so nicely. I shot cows while they were grazing and tried to hit the utter. They didn't like that. I shot frogs that were in great numbers at Lake Washington. It was hard to be really accurate with it, however, because the BB acted a little like a knuckle ball. If the gun were put in a vise and fired repeatedly, the target would look a little like it was hit by a shotgun blast. Once in a while the kids would get carried away and shoot at each other. Even through clothes, it would sting pretty good. Bill got one in the face once and it broke skin right beside his eye.

I was in the back yard and saw a bird sitting on a telephone line. I took a shot at it with my gun at my waist. It hit him with a thud and he fell dead. I went over to him and hoped he wasn't dead, but he was. I wondered how I could hit him when I didn't even aim at him. I felt so badly, I put the gun away for a long time. I bought a BB pistol a few years later from Don Wyland and kept it for many years. It had a nice leather holster but since Don was left handed, it went on the left side of the belt. I hit a lot of targets with it but never killed anything. My compassion for birds and animals was kept a secret for a long time because I didn't want to miss out on the hunting trips. I loved to get out in the country. I went many times and carried a shotgun but never hit anything. Dad thought I was the worst shot he had ever seen. I went with him to Swan Lake which was his favorite place for duck hunting. It was cold and we were hunkered down in the boat behind the blinds that Dad had made. We were having something warm to drink from a thermos when I spotted two teal ducks coming with the wind. I pointed but Dad put down his drink, grabbed his gun, and shot both of them.

Hunting for ducks and pheasants was as important as fishing to my dad. When he wanted to hunt a field, he always got permission from the farmer and sometimes spent a lot of time just talking to him. Grandpa would come from Minneapolis to go pheasant hunting with Dad.

Grandpa and his shotgun

The pheasants were so plentiful the hunters usually went road hunting. This involved driving the country roads until a flock was spotted in a ditch. Hunters would then drive past about a block and stop, sneak up on them and shoot the ones that flew. The daily limits were a real problem so they would sometimes bring a couple home in the hub caps of the car. Dad had more stamina walking the fields than anyone else I saw. The cold didn't seem to bother him either. He would get up early and go duck hunting in the worst weather and sometimes go to work afterwards.

After dark we just hung around and did nothing or we would congregate at someone's house and talk. There was a girl that attracted a few of us on nights when nothing else was going to happen. We would sit on her back steps. She was the only girl that talked to us and as much as I try I can't remember who she was. I can only remember how nice she was and the warm and tranquil feeling I got when I was with her.

Halloween was not a night to be proud of. The younger kids had fun making jack-o-lanterns with candles in them but the older kids were allowed to be destructive without fear of punishment. It was out of control and for a while got worse every year. Anything left out and not tied down would disappear. All cars left out would have all their windows soaped or waxed. When we said, "Trick or treat, money or eat," we meant the trick was to wax windows or something worse if we didn't like the treat. It was a threat. If someone wasn't home, they were treated accordingly. The treats were nothing to brag about either. Popcorn balls were popular and they tasted like they were old. Most candy was hard penny candy with or without wrappers. Sometimes people would give a nickel when they ran out of candy. There was one family in our neighborhood that owned a wholesale candy business. It was the Brockmeier Candy Company. They owned some candy machines around town that were coin-operated. The candy bars in the window of the machine stayed there for a year. When they were changed, they were given out at Halloween. It was a favorite house to get candy but the bars were usually white from the hot summer. We ate them but they weren't very good.

Kids participated long after they were too old. They

used to brag about the damage they had done. Even the beer barrels at the brewery weren't safe. They would be rolled down the hill.

Soaped windows can be washed but waxed windows are hard to clean even with a razor blade. There is only one thing worse and that is wax on a screen. This was good incentive to get the storm windows on by Halloween. I waxed some screens on Graif's house when I became convinced they had called the dogcatcher to pick up my dog, Tippy.

I often wondered why the adults were so tolerant of the kids and came to the conclusion that it was because of the war. The adults had sons, grandsons, or spouses off to war and there was a feeling of protecting the generation that was too young for war.

Some adults were getting tired of the damage and started opening places to go where good things were done. I think it worked after a while and the next generation was a whole lot tamer and today its one of the nicest days for little kids with their costumes.

Whenever a carnival would come to town we would go but didn't spend much money. I watched as others would try to win a stuffed animal but the chances were pretty slim. Throwing balls or rolling balls looked easy but I never tried. Sometimes people would throw coins at a table with cups or dishes and win something based on where the coin stopped. The most fun for us was to go back the next day and try to find coins that were dropped. We didn't find many but it seemed so strange to go back to an empty field where just the day before so many people were enjoying themselves. When the circus came to Mankato, we went over early to get a job putting up the tents. We could earn passes to the show this way. We worked hard and learned some new swear words at the same time. The circus show was not that much even though it was Barnum and Bailey. I'm sure I saw Minnie Pearle and a small band at one of these affairs but that doesn't seem possible. I know I saw her somewhere with that price tag hanging from her hat.

Most summer days we spent at the pool. Except for the time we spent peddling papers, we swam in that cold water. In the morning there was swim classes but the afternoon was open swimming and at night it was open swimming under the lights. It cost a dime each time but we got summer passes. I worked there occasionally handing out baskets for clothes and then retrieving them again when someone turned in a matching number on a safety pin.

Tony, the popcorn man, would bring his popcorn wagon from downtown and park it by the pool each evening. We sometimes had a dime and got some buttered popcorn. He was an institution in Mankato for many years.

Donny was also there every day. He was about 21 years old and was retarded. He could not speak. He would smile and pretend to be shooting ducks with a pretend gun.

The last year I lived on Broad Street I won a trophy for swimming. It took all summer and we raced once per week. My closest rival was Al LaFrance. I was ahead on points until one week I had a cold and my mother said I couldn't go in the cold water. I went to the pool anyway but didn't swim so Al got ahead on points. I thought all was lost but on the last week, his family went on vacation and I won easily. I had that trophy for many years but it was cast out of some pot metal that broke easily and soon it was without arms and eventually it was headless. Even the base was nice. It was made out of walnut.

It was about this time that we discovered that Dad had given all our toys to a friend of his for his kids that didn't have many. When we complained he said that we weren't playing with them anymore. That made some sort of sense but he didn't understand the attachment that we had for them.

There was a bright side to these years too. Comic books were the rage. I don't think I would have learned to read without them. The Dick and Jane schoolbooks just didn't have it. Trading comics was a favorite pastime. We would just go to someone's house and say, "You want to trade comics?", and the negotiations would begin. Some were popular, some were not. You soon learned what they were worth. One *Batman* without a cover could get three *Supermans* in good shape but we didn't want *Superman.* *Flash Gordon, Captain Midnight, The Green Hornet* were popular. Also the funny ones like *Popeye*, and *Mutt and Jeff* brought good trades. *The Lone Ranger* and other cowboy ones weren't worth much. I even read classic comics that were good stories like *The Tale of Two Cities.* We liked to trade with Tom Boyce because he lived in a different neighborhood and had some that we hadn't seen. My folks were good friends with his folks so we drove over there frequently. I also started to read the *Reader's Digest* and we got *Look* or *Life* magazines. I always read the 'Humor in Uniform' first in the *Reader's Digest* and *Look* and *Life* were good for keeping track of the war.

I liked radio a lot more now. Of course, we only had one so you had to listen to the program that someone else chose. The weekly shows were something to look forward to hearing. Even the news was interesting because of the war. I didn't know someone was reading the news. I thought it was someone smart enough to know all that stuff. Listening to the Minnesota Golden Gophers football games was a must. Bernie Bierman was the coach. Bill and I would keep track of every play with a little diagram that showed where the ball was and how it got there. It is hard to describe the excitement and after each game we would have to go outside and play catch with the football.

Special Happenings

When Bill was 10 years old, Mildred took him on a trip to Duluth so 3 years later, Mildred took me to Duluth. That's the way it was suppose to happen. We took the train from Minneapolis to Duluth. My first and last train ride.

We got seats on one of the newest coaches and it was even air-conditioned. The problem was the air conditioning didn't work and worse, there were no windows that opened. It was a very hot day and everyone suffered. I shared a seat with a fat man who took 1 1/2 spaces and sweat like a stuck pig. Going to Duluth was considered a real prize because of all the things to see there. It was an active port on Lake Superior with those huge ore boats coming and going. There were also lift bridges that let the boats through. Just being able to see the lake from high on the hill was wonderful.

Mildred with Bill, Clayt, and Marilyn?

We stayed 3 days and stayed in 3 different hotels. This was not because Mildred liked to see different places but because none of the hotels were up to her expectations. We ate in the dining rooms and went first class. It was a thrill for a 10 year old.

Mildred was easy to criticize because of her mannerisms but she had a heart of gold. We were the only family she had. She was Grandma's half sister. They had the same mother but their fathers were brothers. When Grandma's father died, an unmarried brother in Sweden came to take care of the family as was their custom. Mildred was about 20 years younger and moved in with Grandma and Grandpa when her father died. She was 26 years old and never to marry. I don't think Dad and Irving treated her very well since they were 19 and 14 years old at the time and were used to having the full attention of their folks.

I had a dog and a cat when we lived on Broad Street. They were both strays that I brought home. The dog started following me on my paper route and then would come home with me. My folks told me to call the owners and tell them to keep him in the house when I came by for a few days. The owners told me that it wasn't their dog. He just hung around to eat the food that their cat left. He was a rat terrier and had a crippled back leg. Someone told me it was from a litter of their dog and had fallen down some stairs when he was very little. They said his name was Tippy. (The same one that Graif's turned over to the dogcatcher). I was allowed to keep him but he was not my dad's favorite. Anyway, this little dog followed me everywhere, even when I was on my bike. When we moved to North Mankato at the start of 6th grade he got lost in the shuffle. I didn't know about the dog pound but I'm sure he ended up there.

The cat was in our front yard and wouldn't go away so I fed it. Neither of my folks liked cats but they let me keep her. She used to sleep in bed with me sometimes. She would sneak in after everyone else was asleep. She also had a way of getting into the house from under the front porch to the basement. We called her Kit, short for Kitty, which is what we first called her. She loved to hide in the house and knew of places where we couldn't find her. Once I looked under a bed and saw her tail hanging down from the springs. She got out on the roof one time and couldn't get down, but she got into a basket that we lowered from a window and we pulled her to safety. The dog and cat were not good friends.

We took them both to a cabin that we rented for a week on Lake Washington. They kept us awake during the night with their little spats and I wondered how long my folks were going to put up with my pets and me. Kit got pregnant the next winter and had 5 kittens. The night she got pregnant there were 6 or 8 male cats on our front porch. I chased them away but it was too late. We named the kittens Tiger, Patch, Ears, Boots and Silky Puss. There were two tigers, two with long black and white hair, and one all black one with long silky hair. When we kept them on the back porch, they would go through the holes in the screen and jump to the ground. There they played in the peony bushes and dodged the feet of Matt J. Graif who tried to step on them. Imm's dog got Ears and shook him so badly that Dad put him to sleep with car exhaust. He also made arrangements (without telling me) for a farm to take all except Silky Puss. My folks had started to get attached to this one because of her docile personality. Shortly after however, Dad ran over her with his car. They were afraid to tell me for several days but my calling and searching finally got to them and Mother told me.

My mother was weeding the flowers near the house one-day and uncovered a nest of baby rabbits. She covered it up again and told us about it. We wanted to see them but she said the mother might not come back if she smelled humans on the nest. Shortly after that it was raining and we worried that the nest would fill up with water so we investigated and decided the mother wasn't coming back and we better bring them in the house. They were very tiny and we wondered how to feed them. Ann had a doll bottle that seemed to work just fine. We all took turns feeding them but the milk didn't work and they all died.

Bill broke his leg when I wasn't with him. His explanation of how it happened didn't fool anyone but the truth didn't come out until much later. Bill always chose his friends from the exciting kids his age. Mother said they were wild. One of his friends was Bill Pierce and mother didn't want Bill to hang around with him. Bill told me later that these two were in the second floor of a vacant house when the police came. They had no choice but to jump out the second story window. He got away but it must have hurt pretty good.

He also had an appendicitis attack about this time and the doctor said he barely got to the hospital in time.

During the war it was considered to be 'patriotic' to have a Victory Garden. I can't understand why but maybe it had something to do with transporting goods to town and using gas. Dad went together with his friend, Max Boyce, and rented a vacant lot a couple of blocks away. Dad had the front half and Max had the back. Dad hired someone with a horse to plow ours but Max would spade his by hand. This came as no surprise since he dug a basement under his house with a shovel and a wheel barrel. This block was pretty good size and way too big for a garden. The dirt was black for as deep as you wanted to dig. Dad didn't know much about gardening but planted anyway. We cut up old potatoes and planted several rows. I was surprised they would regenerate from the old pieces. Next we planted several rows of tomatoes. This turned out to be a mistake as you can imagine. We also planted onions, radishes, beans, peas, and cucumbers but no corn. The weeding was done by all of us but nobody liked it. When the potatoes came up they had to be mounded and later the potato bugs were removed by hand. I would carry a jar and crawl along the ground picking bugs and putting them in the jars.

Harvest was the big surprise. We had enough tomatoes and potatoes for a small army. The rest of the stuff was all right but there is something about wasting tomatoes. Bill and I would go everyday and find a couple of bushels of new ripe ones. We had trouble getting them home even using the cart that Bill had built that attached to the bike. Mother was up until midnight everyday boiling, skinning, and canning tomato juice. Bill and I decided to cut down on the size of the crop by one of us throwing them from the plant to the other one on the side walk. Only the ones that survived this without damage were taken home. The potatoes were also too plentiful and many went to waste.

All the big kids smoked so all the little kids wanted to smoke. I think I was addicted before I ever had a cigarette. Dad smoked in the house and the horrible smell seemed to be something that was good. My first remembrance was in 1939. That was the year they built the swimming pool at Tourtellotte park. They also had a kid's hobby shop in the basement. I think it was open only that first year. We didn't make anything down there but it was a place to go to find other kids. Anyway I stood at the top of the stairs on the outside of the door and smoked part of a cigarette. I say part because cigarettes were always hard to come by. We always smoked butts. Some came from Dad's ashtray and some came from the gutter, where cigarettes would come to rest after being thrown out of a car window. The burning end would be knocked off when it hit the ground leaving a lot of good tobacco since they didn't have filter tips. They could be smoked that way or in a pipe. We tried to roll our own with cigarette papers but without much success. Once I got a pipe I could smoke almost anything. I smoked everything that grew in the alley and even coffee smoked pretty good.

Hiding the supply of tobacco was always a problem. I used pipe tobacco tins with cigarette parts hidden in the garage and at strategic places along the paper route.

I didn't smoke everyday from then on but never turned down a chance. I wasn't in real trouble until one of the Peterson kids told me I wasn't really smoking unless I inhaled. That was what I was trying to do when I got dizzy on the water tower. I was about 8 years old.

I got caught smoking at the school picnic at the end of 5th grade. The girls turned us in. The girls were not very sociable. The teacher asked for all my cigarettes and I gave her an opened pack but she knew I had more from her informants. So I had to give up two full packs that I had just bought. One of my classmates had a job in a grocery store where he could steal them. I had the money from the paper route. On the bus ride back to the school I figured she might give them back if I asked for them. When I asked, she said, "We better go visit the principal." Mr. Vistad was a hard-nosed principal and didn't believe my story that they belonged to one of the big kids in the neighborhood who would kill me if I didn't give them back. I told him I was just holding them while he was playing 'horse' with a basketball. I said I forgot to give them back when I left. He asked for the name of the kid and I gave him the name of the oldest kid I knew and he had been smoking for years. As a matter of fact, his nickname was 'One Match Dina' because he could light a cigarette with one match no matter how hard the wind was blowing. Mr. Vistad said he knew the family and would confirm my story with them so he reached for his phone and that was the end of my story. He said he was going to do the worst thing he could think of doing. He said I was going to have to tell my mother and have her call him. That was a relief because I knew I could come up with a story that would satisfy her. But the cigarettes were gone. One pack of Old Golds and one pack of Camels.

My mother was satisfied that I had been hoodwinked into this predicament. I continued to smoke but was more careful about getting caught until my folks knew that I smoked. By the time I was 14, cigarettes were easy to get because I worked at the drug store. I even took a liking to cigars and smoked the 6 cent Headlines. In High School the smokers had to go across the street to smoke but we made no secret of it. In college it was accepted, and when I taught at the University of Minnesota, I would stand under a 'No Smoking' sign at the front of the classroom and light a cigarette. This was used as a sign to the class that it was all right to smoke in class. I wasn't able to quit until I was 30 years old. I tried many times but couldn't get through a day without a cigarette. I finally switched to a pipe for a year before I was able to give that up. I have since read that it may be harder to quit smoking than using heroin. I believe it. My dad never could quit and it killed him.

Part 3

North Mankato

After the episode with the cigarettes at the end of 5th grade, I needed a new start. I got it when we moved to North Mankato. I got new teachers, a new principal, and new friends. North Mankato was a bedroom community for Mankato nestled in the bend of the river. There were about 4,000 or 5,000 residents and a business district several blocks long. One block of the business district had a bakery, drug store, post office, delicatessen, hardware store, bowling alley, and bar. In the adjacent several blocks, there were 5 or 6 bars, two grocery stores, a filling station, and several small businesses mingled among the houses. A couple of blocks away was the public school (grades 1 through 8) and further away was the Catholic school. There were also four or five churches scattered around town. There was one police car and two policemen. The police car had a number 3 on the side as if there were two more. The chief was Fred Quimby and he would ride around town with a German Shepherd police dog during the day and the other policeman got the night shift. At 10:00PM a siren would blow indicating a curfew. We all knew what that meant but paid no attention to it.

The House at 601 Wall Street

Dad had always wanted to own a house and his folks lent him the 25% down payment that was required. In some ways it wasn't as good a house as the one we left. It had only one bathroom and three bedrooms. Bill and I had to share a bedroom with rollaway beds. The house was on the corner but had a house between it and the alley so there wasn't much of a back yard. It had a small single car garage attached to the house with an unheated hallway connecting it to the kitchen. The basement had a cistern but it was no longer used because there was a built in water softener. The house had a coal furnace with gravity feed much like the house on 4th Street.

A Recent Photo of 601 Wall St.

I wasn't too familiar with North Mankato so I was told how to get there. I was told to go south on Broad Street for 15 blocks to Main Street. Then I was to go west across the railroad tracks and bridge over the river to North Mankato. Why wasn't this called West Mankato, I asked? Well, I was told there was already an area of town with that name. It was south of Main Street. There was no South Mankato, thank goodness. Years later when I saw a map of Mankato I could see that it followed the river which did swing to the west after it went south of Main Street. This means there is a part of town that is west and from there one can look north across the river to North Mankato so I suppose one has to know what part of town was settled first to make sense of this.

Crossing the bridge was no problem except it was pretty cold in the winter. The bridge was an important thing. It was the only way to get from North Mankato to Mankato for many miles and there were always people walking across it. During the summer, people would fish for catfish off the side and during the spring we would gather to watch the big chunks of ice slam into the supports and shake the bridge.

Getting across the railroad tracks was often a problem because the trains would switch there. One man with a stop sign was all that controlled the traffic. I think it was the same guy for many years.

I kept my paper route in the 'north end' of town so I still had my friends there. This made the transition easier for me. Shortly after I moved to North Mankato, Junior Brant hanged himself. He was a friend who lived down the street on Broad St. I used to trade comics with him and he had a supply of those little pictures (transfers) we could put on our skin that looked like tattoos. We had to trade for them with marbles or comic books. No one knew why he hanged himself but some said it was because the cast on his broken leg was bothering him. I doubted that.

Sixth Grade

I was sent off to School armed with a report card that said I had passed 5th grade. There was no advanced registration necessary; they just took the kids that showed up. The school was old and even had a bell tower with a working bell.

I found the 6th grade teacher and told her I was new there and she said that she was too. That seemed to help.

Actually there were two 6th grade teachers. Mine

was Virginia Rettke and she was blonde and 19 or 20 years old. She was fresh out of Mankato State Teacher's College that had a two-year program for elementary teachers. She

Recent Photo of North Mankato School

was not only young but good looking. She had frequent visitors at school sometimes in Navy uniforms. She would go out in the hall to talk to them and we would get loud so she would come back in and say, "Cllllaaaaasss." That meant to shut up. The other sixth grade teacher's name was Miss Appledorn and she was also right out of college. She was a little taller and red headed. Sometimes they would combine the classes for things like tumbling. We used to get

Miss Appledorn to help us learn to stand on our head. She would grab our ankles and we would peek up her skirt.

I sat toward the back on the row by the windows. There was a bookcase there and a radiator. The bookcase had a small library of things to read when I wasn't paying attention to the teacher. I liked the Don Winslow books the best. Phil Cowan sat right in front of me. I was playing with a wire clothes hanger one day and decided to heat it up on the radiator and see if I could get Phil's attention with it. That wouldn't have been so bad but at the last minute I decided to loop it over the radiator and pull back and forth to add a little frictional heat. When I put it on Phil's neck, it scorched him pretty good. He let out a yelp and the teacher came to see what was wrong. He had tears in his eyes but insisted that everything was all right. I found out Phil was just one of many good kids in North Mankato.

We also had one boy in our class that was definitely retarded. He wasn't dangerous or disruptive but he paid no attention to anything that the rest of us were doing in class. He tried to amuse us with his antics but he wasn't funny. When his brother died in a tractor accident, we saw him all dressed up. He said he was going to his brother's funeral and was proud of his cloths. He had no comprehension of death. I think his name was Jim Starrett.

Not only were the guys more friendly but so were the girls. I didn't have any that lived near my house but they were out walking around in bunches and we would join them and end up at one of their houses. We ended up in a tree once and had a kissing party. Dolly Overlea and Ardis Snitzler were there and maybe some others too. We often went to Dolly's house because we could play in her garage. Her mother didn't have a car which sounds pretty sad but lots of people didn't have cars and they got along just fine. Girls were always at the skating rink in winter and we skated with them with one arm around them. I was beginning to like North Mankato even if it was misnamed.

There were some guys that didn't welcome me with

open arms. Bob Kulseth, Duane Swan, and Dennis Lindeen felt they controlled my neighborhood and didn't need help from me. When I first met them they were at Bob's house so I stopped on my bike to talk. They were sitting on the curb and started throwing pebbles at my bike wheel. When that didn't get a reaction from me they threw bigger stones that probably left their mark. They were trying to start a fight but that wasn't my favorite pastime so I didn't bite. When they asked why I didn't care about my bike I told them it belonged to my older brother. That sank in and the stones stopped. Later I played on the same basketball team with them and found them to be nice guys.

Don Wyland lived across the street and up a few doors. He was nice to me right away even though he was a year older. He taught me to play chess so we spent quite a few hours together on his front porch.

On D-day, June 6, 1944, I was in the dentist's chair listening to a radio. My dentist was Dr. Claude Waldo Moulten and he was preparing to put braces on my teeth. He wasn't an orthodontist but his brother was. There wasn't an orthodontist in town and he agreed to put the braces on my teeth. Our other dentist was Dr. Haas and he had referred us to Dr. Moulten who had an office just down the hall in the Brett Building. My brother had braces too but I can't remember if he got his first. My teeth were the worst. I had my grandmother's mouth with a narrow upper palate and a huge overbite. My grandmother had all her teeth pulled out when she was 16 years old because it was so bad.

I didn't know what D-day meant but Dr. Molten explained what was going on as he listened to the radio. He was very excited and he stuttered when he was excited but he got the message across. This was the first of many visits to him at great expense. Not only for the braces but my teeth were decaying under the bands and wires and had to be filled first with silver and later with gold. All this cost a lot of money and I heard about it each month when Dad paid the bills. I think it was Mother's idea that we all get braces, but it meant the end of my trombone playing. By the time my sister was ready for braces the orthodontists knew that they had to pull some teeth to make room for others in a mouth that was too small. In my case they just pushed and pulled with no lasting effect. It went on for years. I even had a removable retainer with a huge wedge that made my jaw slide forward when I closed my mouth. It was longer than my front teeth. When I went to a new school in 9th grade, I was sent to speech class where they politely told me I couldn't say my th's. I took out my retainer and said I could do it without that in my mouth which embarrassed the speech teacher. I was sent back to regular class.

De-tasseling corn was one of the ways I could earn money; enough money to justify paying my substitute to peddle the papers. It was hard work and long hours out in the hot fields. At first we tried to take off our shirts to keep cool and to get a sun tan but that was a mistake. The corn had a way of slicing your skin like a paper cut. Kids always fight and this place was no exception. Ken Beavens and one of the Ramy brothers were fighting and rolling on the ground and I thought that this job was hard enough without exerting energy in a fight like that. Ken wore a big straw cowboy hat so we called him cowboy. We were bused to and from the fields and told what rows to work by a boss. There were teams of girls doing it too. There was talk about the girls doing it topless and we might run into them down a row. I knew if we couldn't take our shirts off, they couldn't either. It was easier if you were tall like I was so I wondered how the shorter girls could have done it.

Another way to make money was to pick strawberries. I tried that only once. We were driven out of town about 10 miles to a farm that had large patches of strawberries. We were to be paid by the pint and were given a flat that held 6 pint-boxes. Leaning over to pick anything by the ground was not to my liking but it was for money. I couldn't help but keep track of how many I had picked and how long it took so I could determine how much I could make in a day. When I got my first flat of 6 pints picked I went to the lady in charge to get credit for them. She took one pint and spread it over the others so I got credit for only 5 pints. This made me angry and I talked to others who had gotten the same treatment. We continued picking and wondering what we were going to do about it. Finally at noon we all quit. We worried about getting back home so we decided to quit early enough so we could walk home if necessary and it was necessary. We walked for miles across country thinking that was the shortest distance but none of us knew where we were. After a long time we came to highway 14 but still were a long way from home so we tried to hitchhike, without success. There were too many of us so everyone got down in the ditch except one or two and when a car would stop, we would appear. Somehow we all got back all right. After hearing the story my dad drove me out to the farm the next Saturday and demanded the money I had coming. They gave it to him.

Home and Family

When Ann got Scarlet Fever we were all affected. Our house was quarantined. The Public Health Officer nailed a sign on our house and we were stuck there for 14 days. Dad moved out so he could go to work. The milkman would bring milk but couldn't take the empties until the sign came down. Bill and I sneaked out once to watch bowling. Dad had arranged for us to go to the bowling alley and watch through the window that was used to show movies when the building was a movie theater. Later the doctor thought she might have Rheumatic Fever so she wasn't allowed to do anything. She was told to stay in bed most of the time. Corky (our dog) stayed with her like he was the sick one. She missed so much school there was talk about holding her back a year but Bill and I argued against it. We thought it would be too hard on her ego.

I always enjoyed making people laugh. It was a thing I tried hard to perfect. I told lots of canned jokes but my mother said she didn't think that any of them were funny. She had a good sense of humor but it had to be extemporaneous. I saved my best stuff for the dinner table and if I timed it just right I could get Bill to laugh with his mouth full. He would choke and sometimes milk would come out his nose.

I was always too thin and was self-conscious about it. I was growing too fast and it was easy to slouch to cover up the embarrassing fact that I stuck out like a sore thumb. My dad would not allow this, however, and would say, "Stand up straight," at least once a day. At the table, he would say, "Sit up straight and lean over your plate." I had trouble doing that.

I had to be called twice for dinner because I was never hungry. I didn't care much for Mom's cooking but I guess she cooked for my dad. He liked things like liver, boiled spare ribs, pickled pig's feet, sour kraut, boiled cabbage, etc. I had a different idea of what tasted good. I liked her hash that she made from left over meat that was sent through the grinder, left over potatoes and onions all fried in a big cast iron frying pan. I also liked her hot dish that she called goulash. The problem with this was that she never measured anything and sometimes it was much better than other times. If we really liked something and asked her to do it again she couldn't reproduce it because she didn't know how much of anything she had put in it. She did a good job of fixing Dad's ducks and pheasants. She made soup, however, that she called stew and it was awful. It contained cooked vegetables, including cabbage, and little pieces of meat. I could raise a spoonful to my mouth but my stomach would wretch as soon as I smelled it and I couldn't swallow. I would sit at the table for hours with the instruction that I couldn't leave until I had finished it. I was skin and bone and they thought I was just stubborn about eating. Mom also had a problem with making gravy and white sauce. She thought that if she added flour to water, it would mix by itself. The gravy was always lumpy but on special occasions she would strain it. She used the white sauce on scalloped potatoes with the same result every time. The potatoes would be separated by little balls of white sauce that would pop into pure flour when you separated them.

I did drink a lot of milk and mother complained about the cost so one of us found out about the skim milk that was available at the Model Dairy for 10 cents a gallon. We had to supply our own container so I would ride my bike to the dairy with a glass gallon jug in each of my forefingers. Coming home was more difficult but it was only two blocks. I never dropped one.

When Dad's 1936 Ford started to wear out he bought a used 1938 DeSoto. The war was on and they weren't making new cars. When we first took it out for a ride we were all surprised at how much better a 'big' car would ride and, of course, it had good brakes. The back seat was no warmer than the old one, however.

It was the only car we had and when it was in for repairs, we walked. It was in repair for months once when Dad hit a hay wagon. He was coming home from hunting after dark when he hit a horse drawn hay wagon. He hit it in the rear and it tore off the right side of the car. The post between the two doors was bent right up to the ceiling. Ordinarily the car would have been totaled but there was such a shortage of cars that it was rebuilt. The engine was rebuilt at 50,000 miles because that was about all one could get out of an engine. It didn't start very well in the cold before or after the overhaul.

Dad was a complex person who liked to hunt and fish like a sportsman but at the same time was the three-piece suit type that fit in as a Standard Oil manager. He was very neat and orderly especially when it came to clothes. He had many suits but worried that he didn't have the right colored one when he was asked to be a pallbearer for Mr.

Peters. He usually wore a tie even on vacations as can be seen in the picture on page 51. He also was an artist and could play the accordion but he hung out at the bars after work. He could draw cartoons and had a couple appear in magazines like *Look* and *Life*.

He actually drew them for *The Duration Digest*, which was the magazine that Standard Oil published for their employees in the service. When the cartoons appeared in the big magazines Dad wrote and asked them how they could do that without his permission. He was told that *The Duration Digest* wasn't copyrighted. Dad used to curl also. He was in a league that curled in an unheated rink. We went to watch a couple of times even though we didn't know the rules of the game. I got the biggest bang out of watching the sweepers with their long corn brooms cleaning the ice to control the ball.

He didn't like to go to church but always felt guilty about it. We joined a different church in North Mankato thinking that might help. The Minister came to visit us unexpectedly shortly after we joined but it happened at the worst possible time. It was one of the few times Dad had had too much to drink and was upstairs in the bathroom getting sick. Mother could have made an excuse but she had no sympathy for him. Instead she called for him to come down and meet 'our' company. He came down and put up a good show but that must have been the longest hour in his life. We didn't go to the new church either.

The only other time I saw him drunk was when he fell down our stairs. He was going up to bed and his feet got ahead of his body and he fell over backwards. At the bottom of the stairs he hit the wardrobe. This caused him to break his glasses that in turn cut a flap in his forehead about the size of a 50 cent piece. I was already in bed when I heard the commotion. When I got downstairs I saw Dad on the floor bleeding and Mother was sitting in a chair stomping her feet and screaming. Corky was there licking up the blood. I thought I better find something for Mother to do so

I told her to call Dad's doctor. After some time she was able to do this but when she hung up I asked what he was going to do and she said that we should put a Band-Aid on it. I knew that wasn't going to work so I called him, with some difficulty, and told him to come over. He agreed and came in about 1/2 hour. Dad hadn't moved and we were afraid to move him. When the doctor came in he looked at Dad while taking off his coat, and said, "Get up, Ken, you look like hell down there." So Dad got up and they went to the hospital to get his cut sewed up. He spent the night there so he must have been in tough shape.

Clayt, Ann, and Corky

Corky

Corky would deserve mention in anyone's book. He was a real character. He was my dad's dog when it was time to go hunting, my dog when it was time to go to school and Bill's, Ann's or Mom's when they wanted a dog. Mr. Sjodin gave him to my dad as payment for rides to work. Bill and I walked to Sjodin's garage to pick him out of a litter of pups. The mother was a Springer Spaniel but the father was known only as a traveling salesman. The litter was in the garage and poured out when we opened the door. It was hard to pick one because they all looked alike and acted the same. Then we noticed one was still in the garage. We said, "What is the matter with him?" There was nothing wrong with him. He was just different so he came home with us. I don't know how old he was but he had an awful time getting up the curbs from the street. He kept bumping his chin.

He grew up in a hurry. Especially with the food my dad would fix for him. There was usually some dog food in a meal but mostly it was scraps of people food carefully arranged in his bowl and often with gravy of some sort over the top. Once when he was very small we went to visit our grandparents in Minneapolis. Somehow two people fed him without the other knowing. He dutifully ate both meals. When we realized what had happened we took him outside for fear he would explode. His stomach touched the ground but he didn't get sick.

Hunting was his passion. Dad taught him to retrieve ducks and pheasants and how to sweep back and forth in a field. He could not resist going after rabbits, however, in spite of all my dad's efforts. I only went duck hunting with them once but I saw Corky retrieve not only the ducks that Dad shot but any other wounded ones in the area. He got pretty good at getting pheasants too. He would catch them if they wouldn't fly. He refused to retrieve a hen pheasant that my dad had shot and we said he was smarter than my dad. We weren't allowed to shoot hens but Dad had promised the farmer that we would leave any that were shot by mistake at the farmhouse. At the end of a day of hunting Corky was a mess. He was full of burrs and mud and usually too tired to get back in the car. Dad had a tarp to cover the back seat and we would lift him in so he could ride home like a hero. Before hunting season would start, Dad would get the guns out to oil them. When Corky saw this he would sit by Dad and quiver.

I would take him squirrel hunting along the hills north of town. It was a beautiful place especially in the fall. The leaves would be ankle deep and the whole place would take on a yellow color. I didn't often go alone because there was usually someone willing to go. I liked to go with someone like Phil Cowan because he would take the squirrels home for his mother to cook. We would shoot them out of trees and Corky would be there when they hit the ground. He would give them a shake and bring them to me. I found out later they could hit the ground and run away if you didn't have a dog like Corky to break their necks.

Corky had the run of the town and showed up at my school every day. He didn't necessarily follow me there. He was just there. He and about seven other dogs were there. They didn't stay there all day but were always there when school let out for the day. When I graduated from 8th grade, Mr. Dubke said he should have a perfect attendance award and made some mention about me not getting close to one. Corky usually went to the all-school functions, as well. There was no auditorium in our school so we had to march across the street to the municipal building for our all-school functions. When we did this, the two doors to the municipal building were propped open. This was an invitation to Corky to come sit by me in my assigned spot. He didn't

Recent Photo of Municipal Building

come in right away but waited until we were ready to start the program. I guess he thought there was less chance of getting thrown out that way.

In the summer he had a habit of taking naps right in the middle of our intersection. The cars had no trouble avoiding him but the bus barely had room to get around so the drivers would honk at him, but to no avail.

His life wasn't without accidents and injury. Once I saw him get hit by a car. I was at Skip's and was going home across Belgrade Ave. I started across but stopped when I saw a car coming. He didn't stop and was hit broadside. The bumper of the car knocked him to one side so he wasn't run over. He lay in the gutter and I thought he was dead. Skip came and thought the same thing. After a little while he got up and could walk but wouldn't come across the street with me. I had to carry him across the street but then he was fine.

One day we got a call from a neighbor who told us Corky was on their front porch and badly hurt. My dad and I went with the car to get him and decided he might have been shot because he was bleeding on both sides at about the shoulder. We were afraid to move him but managed to roll him onto an old piece of carpet and carried him to the car.

We got him home and carried him to the basement this way. Dad then called a veterinarian to come to our house. The vet looked him over pretty good and decided he wasn't hurt very much. He gave Corky a slap and told him to get up. Corky growled at him and he backed off. The vet thought maybe a cat had ridden on his back and scratched him on both sides. Anyway Corky could not get up the stairs for a couple of weeks and we didn't mind carrying him. He forgot one day and came up to the landing by himself so that game was over. He pulled the same stunt when he had a problem with an ear. He loved the attention it got him. We had to put salve in it a couple of times a day and he walked with that ear nearly touching the ground. For a long time after that we could ask him, "How is your ear?" and he would put it down near the ground and walk funny.

We would have to give him capsules every once in a while and he didn't like taking them. I tried putting them in the middle of a small ball of hamburger and tossing it to him. He would catch it, gulp it down, and then spit out the clean capsule.

He didn't discover girl dogs for a long time but from then on he was trying to make up for lost time. I think it was Uncle Irving's dog, Jiggs, who taught him. We were visiting them once when the two dogs took off together and didn't come back at bedtime. In the middle of the night Aunt Rufine heard Corky at the back door and went to let him in. She waited for Jiggs to come in but he wasn't there. After a few minutes Corky asked to go back out again. Rufine said that evidently he had only come back for a drink of water.

He would often sit for hours watching a house where there was a dog in heat; even in the middle of winter. Once he didn't come home and Dad was afraid to leave him out for the night because it was so cold. I told Dad where Corky had been seen watching a house so he went over there. He came home without Corky and said he had been sitting there so long his hair was frozen in the ice. Dad got a pair of scissors and went back for him. He looked pretty funny for a while with his shanks all cut off.

He had a nasty habit of bringing someone else's garbage home from the garbage cans in the alley. He looked so proud coming along the sidewalk with a bag in his mouth. He never opened it until he got to our side yard. I don't know what he ate but he always left the eggshells and coffee grounds for me to clean up. One day he brought home a whole pound of butter. We worried about where he had gone to get that.

When I was in 9th and 10th grade, I would walk across the bridge to Mankato to go to the YMCA where a lot of kids hung out. Corky used to follow me but I didn't want him with me. He didn't walk with me but stayed back a couple of blocks and pretended to be checking out the shrubs and stuff. Then when I was a long way from home, he would appear as if by chance seeing me. He knew I wouldn't take him home from there. I could ditch him by going in the side door of the Saulpaugh Hotel and coming out the front. Corky would wait patiently until I would come home by going through the hotel in the reverse order. Once I got a ride home and forgot about him. When he wasn't home at bedtime Dad asked me if I knew where he was. I told him and he drove over to get Corky by the side door. Corky seemed surprised that I was home when he got there. I don't think he ever trusted me fully again.

Corky probably saved my life one night. Lin Barnes and I wanted to stay out late so we told our parents we were going to camp out. We put up a tent on the hill not too far from his house. We then went to the function that we wanted to attend. Corky was with us so he must have gone to the function, as well. When we went to the tent to sleep, it was pitch dark and the tent was hard to find. We were walking up the hill looking for it when we heard horses running toward us. Corky started barking and the horses stopped. The next morning we looked at the situation and decided that the horses could have run over us and maybe continued over the edge of a steep cliff that could have killed them as well.

He didn't like Jo right away. When we would go over to the house to watch TV he would sit between us and sometimes when I would go to the kitchen for something he would growl at Jo. He had a nasty growl and she was afraid of him. I knew him to be all bluff and thought it was funny.

I moved away after college and didn't see him much. Once I came to visit after being away for about 6 months and he greeted me like he always did. He would run straight at me and at the last second I would step aside and grab his front leg so he would roll over and over. Then he would get up and run at me again until we both tired of it.

Bowling

I went bowling once before moving to North Mankato. I had to demonstrate my four-step delivery to my dad before he would take me. I did pretty well for the first time and I knew I was going to like to bowl for a long time. When we moved to North Mankato there was a bowling alley just two blocks away. It had been a movie theater but Bill Tanley bought the bowling alleys where I first bowled and moved them to the theater building. Bill Tanley lived just a half a block away in a house much like ours. His mother and sister lived across the street in a house that he owned. He seemed to own quite a few businesses around town and the ballpark was even named Tanley Field. At the beginning of the war he owned a pop bottling plant and several beer distributorships. The story was told that he was buying extra sugar before it was rationed. One of his truck drivers was delivering the sugar when he tipped over and spilled the sugar onto the street. Sugar hoarding was against federal law so he was convicted. It is said that he was sentenced to some jail time but was allowed to spend the time at his retreat in northern Minnesota. He lost these businesses including the Hamm's Beer Distributorship. He was now active in running the bowling alley.

The bowling alley was a nice place to hang around because there were lots of seats and there was a cafe in the front. The sound of the pins going down was always associated with fun to me. There were always kids there waiting to set pins but there were some adult pin- setters also. Bill Miexner was the manager and he would select the pin-setter when someone came in to bowl. There didn't seem to be any sort of system.

I soon got a chance to learn how to set pins. I think we got 6 cents per line. There was nothing automatic about it. One had to pick up the pins and put them in the rack and then put all your weight on the bar that lowered the rack. We would pick up several pins in each hand with the pins between the fingers. At first this would cause blisters that soon popped. The pins were released when the rack touched the alley. The ball was put on the rail and sent back to the bowler. Two alleys shared a ball rail so the two pin-setters had to be careful not to put the balls too close together for the trip back. It was a hard job and wasn't very safe. The pins often flew out of the pits so we would sit with our feet up on the pin rack. That way we would get hit only on the back of the legs from these errant pins. I soon learned which spare combinations would lead to flying pins. Sometimes a bowler would double ball you, which meant he would throw a different ball at a spare without waiting for the first ball to be back in place. A pin-setter would be standing in the pit picking up pins when the second ball would come. After hollering at the bowler we would sometimes throw the ball back up the alley at him. I did most of my pin setting before I was 14 so we were always on the lookout for the guys that were looking for violations of the child labor laws. When we were warned that they were on their way back to the pits, we would go out the back door leaving the bowlers without half the setters. During the time I was setting pins they installed semi-automatic pin- setters. These looked the same but the rack would go down and set the pins when the setter pulled a rope. This little addition allowed one setter to handle two lanes. Julian Klugerts was one of the adult setters and was very different. He was slightly dwarfed and had huge eyeteeth. He was not dumb as some thought but was something of an arithmetical whiz. He always knew what frame we were in and checked the team additions after each league. After I turned 14, I agreed to be interviewed by the inspectors as if I was a regular pin-setter. I felt pretty grown up and happy to be of help.

Setting pins was not nearly as much fun as bowling. As pin-setters, we got to bowl free on Saturday mornings if we set pins for each other. One ball (number 72) was lighter than the others and had small finger holes. I used that ball whenever it was available. I tried to throw a curve ball but without any luck until I tried a 2- fingered ball. It was so hard to hold that I got a natural curve just by the way it fell out of my hand. I started bowling in a league as soon as I could hold an average of about 150. At first I bowled 2nd shift (from 9:00 - 11:00) because that was for the bowlers with the biggest handicaps.

Bowling was a passion for Dad all his life. I saw him play baseball once and I saw him curl in the winter. He was a pretty good bowler but never as good as he wanted to be. He liked to bowl pot games with the best bowlers in town but struggled to stay even. Going to tournaments out of town was always big with him. Bill and I used to watch him and the other good bowlers every week. We knew the team standings at all times and Dad was usually the secretary for the league so we helped him do the books each week. He also did cartoon characterizations of the members of the winning bowling team in the league where he bowled. The teams were all sponsored by bars and the drawing would be put up in the bar. One of our favorite pastimes was to imitate the different bowlers. They all had distinctive styles and we could do them all from 3-step Kenny King to 5-step Don Rebstock.

Bowling pins were made of maple so even the worn

out ones were nice. We had some old ones at home for burning in the furnace but we played with them first. In the winter, when the streets were covered with snow, we would set them up in the street and roll other pins at them. It was fun to hear the noise and see them go down.

Don Rebstock was one of the best bowlers in town but some people thought Vic Buckholz was better. The debate went on for a long time and finally a big match was arranged. Vic threw a straight ball and never missed a spare. Don threw a mean hook but had more trouble with spares. The pressure was extreme as we could see from the way they were sweating. I suppose big money was bet on the match but no one talked about that. I was there but I can't remember who won.

Bowling tournaments were the highlight of both watching and participating. There was a formality involved that raised the level of excitement. New pins were used that made high scores difficult and official scorers kept track of the scores in addition to the overhead scoring. The bowlers were more serious, too, because they had to put up money to get in the tournament and everyone at least expected to get their money back. I bowled in a few tournaments out of town and didn't want to take a chance of finding a ball at the alley that would fit so I borrowed Al Meyer's ball. He owned Meyer's Drug Store and was known as a good guy so I wasn't afraid to ask him for his ball. It was a 2-finger ball very close to the one I used in town. The ABC tournament came to Minneapolis and our team went. The pageantry was impressive. We even had to have our balls weighed before the tournament began. None of us bowled any better in the tournaments than we did in leagues except Jerry Dutler. He did well in all tournaments but he won the coveted Peterson classic in Chicago. I think it paid $12,000. The most significant thing about this win was that the alley conditions were notoriously bad. I bowled with Jerry many times as a kid and didn't think he would ever be good because he raised the ball above his head on the approach. How wrong I was.

After the War

When the Japanese surrendered it was a feeling of great relief. The end of the war with Germany had been expected for some time but the feeling was that beating Japan was going to be a lot harder. There was a great expectation that things would be back to normal overnight. When that didn't happen there was a period of let down. Shortages appeared when rationing ended. Inflation was so bad that price controls were put into effect. Labor unions went on strike everywhere making matters worse. New cars were in such short supply that one had to get on a waiting list and if you got one, it might not have all it's parts. Dick Ryan's dad got a Nash with a 4x4 wooden bumper. There were price controls in effect for new cars so many were driven around the block and sold as used cars with a higher price than new ones. The war had some subtle effects that we didn't see at the time. For instance, a lot of family photographs were taken before the war and after, but very few during it.

This all came at a bad time for my dad because Grandpa died unexpectedly just a few weeks before the war ended and Grandma was in poor health with circulatory problems and diabetes. This marked an end to most of our Minneapolis visits and made Dad a harder person to live with. I often felt sorry for Mother. I spent less and less time at home as did Bill.

Seventh Grade

Seventh grade was the start of Junior High and it meant we had several teachers. We would walk in line from one room to the other but the break every hour was welcomed. By that time I knew Ken Uhlhorn, John Kolling, Jim Taylor, Dick Ryan, and Lloyd Horness. We were starting to feel our oats and were becoming something of a problem in school. I knew the other kids too, of course, but we were the most outspoken ones. One of our teachers quit after a short time and we got Mrs. Olive Anderson to finish out the year. She knew how to handle us without getting excited. She would raise her eyebrows to signal enough. We had Miss Lambert for math and Mrs. Sjodin for English. Mr. Dubke was the principal and taught shop. Clair Hoehne was the physical education teacher and coach. He thought physical education was calisthenics and coaching was shouting. He spent a lot of time teaching the boys and girls how to dance the Lindy. Of course, the boys and girls were on opposite sides of the gym. Mrs. Sjodin's husband worked with Dad at Standard Oil so I had to behave in her class. She had a good sense of humor and laughed so hard at something I said that she bent over in her chair and threw her pencil. I think it was that year that we were studying science and the book said it was possible that man could get to the moon by the year 2000. I calculated that I would be 67 years old and thought, "I hope I live long enough to see that happen." In History I was told about the rise and fall of the Roman Empire. I couldn't understand why they didn't stop it from falling after it became obvious it was going down hill.

At the beginning of 7th grade I met Skip. Actually it was Dewey Rasdall that said to me, "Did you see Skip smile at you?" and I said, "Who is Skip?" He told me her name was actually Marilyn Phillipson and he pointed her out. She was in 8th grade so I was surprised. I waited until we passed in the hall going from class to class and sure enough she did smile. I found out she lived right across the street from the school so I waited on the school grounds for her to come back to school after lunch. I spoke to her several times this way but I was too shy to do anything else. Then I noticed something. She smiled at everyone like that. This came as a blow to me but I was hooked anyway.

This made it pretty difficult but I continued to go out of my way to talk to her and she was always polite.

Someone had the bright idea of publishing a one-page school newspaper with all the gossip that was around. I made the paper as Skip's biggest pest. I wondered if she was behind it. I gave it up for a while but I always wanted the things I couldn't have. One day during Christmas vacation I walked down to the skating rink and saw her. She came over to me and said, "Why don't you go home and get your skates?" so I did. I skated with her and walked home with her carrying her skates. That winter I spent a lot of time with her on her front porch trying to forget how cold it was. When we couldn't stand the cold anymore she would go in and I would walk home on numb feet. We got along fine but I was still shy and didn't have enough nerve to kiss her until the next fall. She was everything I could want. She had dark hair and put it up in bobby pins every night so the ends were always curly. She had a pretty face and that quick smile. She wrote me a letter when I was at Scout Camp. I took her for granted about then and wasn't always nice to her. She wanted me to come to her piano recital but I refused. I let her run home alone when we were over at Joan Guth's house and she realized she was late getting home. I didn't go over to her house as often because I was doing so many other things. I got a flat top hair cut about that time as an expression of defiance. Mother hated it and so did Skip. It was called a 'heinie' because the German soldiers all had them. I guess that's why these haircuts were so disliked.

It wasn't long before she started noticing other boys especially the new ones she met in 9th grade. She asked me if she could go out with them and I knew it was over. I stalled it off for a little while but she wasn't interested in me any more. I saw her once in a while after that but she was always going with someone else.

I loved shop for the next three years. We learned how to use all the power equipment and made little things to take home. My first project was a corner shelf that required the use of the power jig saw (scroll saw) to cut the sides. Even sanding and finishing seemed like fun at the time. The paint room smelled so strong that Dick Ryan and I decided to fake sickness and go home. We actually planned to get our guns and skip school for the rest of the day. We did all that and had a wonderful time in the woods north of town. We didn't expect that our homeroom teacher would ask for excuses from home. After all we did get sick in school. When she did ask for an excuse, we said, "Oh, we will get one tomorrow." She finally stopped asking. I think they all knew. That must have been in 8th grade and we were getting pretty close to graduation.

Boy Scouts

Shortly after I turned 12 years old I joined the Boy Scouts. It was the lower age limit at that time. Bill had tried the Scouts years before but didn't like it. Maybe the troop had a lot to do with it. Mine was Troop 29 of North Mankato and it was a good one. The older kids ran it and there was no parent involvement. There were a few adults that helped but mostly we were on our own. We met every Wednesday at the municipal building but also had access to the school shop. The PTA was our sponsor but gave us no money. The money for our equipment and camps was earned by us, mostly by paper drives. We didn't have any competition and the lumberyard would donate a truck. Once we were going around town on one of the paper drives when we came to Dr. Nilson's house. Mrs. Nilson was waiting for us with lots of paper and a bunch of old medical books. She told us emphatically that we were not to look in the medical books because the pictures were for doctor's eyes only. Now why would she have told us all that?

For me, the Scouts filled several needs. First it was organized like the military with the uniforms, medals for accomplishments, army style caps, and leaders that gave orders, etc. With the war coming to an end without my involvement, the Scouts became the next best thing. We learned Morse Code, tied knots, learned first aid, and marched. We also sang songs and told stories.

It was also like the military where you started out at the bottom (a tenderfoot) and worked your way up with time and training. Each advancement was tested and you were given your award at a huge gathering of the Council, called a Court of Honor.

Our Wednesday nights had a routine to them that was followed and we knew what to expect. We did things by patrol and we had 4 of them with about 10 scouts in each. Each one had a patrol leader and an assistant patrol leader. We lined up, saluted the flag, took attendance and were told what we were going to do that night. Then we spent time learning some new first aid practice or knot tying. After that we went to the stage and set up the campfire (artificial) and sat around it for story telling and singing campfire songs. When that was over, there would be a meeting of the leaders (the green bar meeting) and the rest would play basketball or protect the lights. This game involved dividing the group into two parts with one surrounding the light switches. When the lights were turned off, it got completely dark and the other half of the group was suppose to turn them back on with no rules. It was better than basketball and everyone got to participate.

Camping out was the big thing in scouting. Getting away from home was the best part. Not that it was that bad, but there was no independence at home. Even sleeping in a tent in the yard was fun at first.

When we weren't camping we were preparing for the next outing or cleaning up from the last one. I wasn't prepared for my first camp. I didn't have any equipment. I didn't even have a uniform which was all right because you had to earn the right to wear one. I started with a shirt and added a little at a time because we had to buy everything from Fishers, a local men's store. Since I had no sleeping bag I asked Mother to help me put together a bedroll. I think it consisted of a flannel sheet and an army blanket. I'm not sure what time of year it was but I was so cold that I didn't sleep at all. Our tents had no floors and we had to sleep on the ground. It was still a thrill.

Free Time Activities

Most free time activities were unplanned but when we had some free time we never stayed at home and never did homework. We would just go out and hope to run into someone else. Sometimes when I was walking somewhere in the evening, I would feel so good that I would break into a run and run as far as I could.

There were the good places to go like the bowling alley, the ice rink, the park, but often times it was just running into someone by luck. We didn't do much after we got together but it was still fun. In the fall we would carry a salt shaker and go stealing apples. Once around Christmas time I was out walking while it was snowing. I had recently heard the Christmas song that contains 'let it snow, let it snow' and it was going round and round in my head. I met up with other kids and we were standing under a street light watching it snow and it seemed so perfect. I remember Dolly was there.

The dump in North Mankato was a small area down by the river that was unattended. People could leave anything there and often something that was unwanted by one person was taken home by another. There was always a small fire or two smoldering there and the rats ate any edibles that were left. Garbage was handled separately. A farmer who fed it to pigs picked it up. The small size of the dump spoke to the frugality of the 4,000 or so inhabitants of the town. They didn't throw many things away. Shooting rats with a .22 was fun and not that easy. They were pretty wary once the shooting began. They could hide in the cans and bottles pretty well. We were usually content to shoot bottles. We also blew up bottles with firecrackers. It was even more fun to put a lighted firecracker in a bottle and throw it up in the air to see it explode in the air. This backfired on me when a firecracker went off just as I released a catsup bottle. It showered me with glass and catsup. I wore glasses then and they took a blow from a piece of glass without breaking. It made my nose sore but probably saved an eye. It wasn't until I got home and washed off the catsup that I determined that I only had a few small cuts on my face.

The dump wasn't the only place by the river where we played. We had access to the river several places and played down there quite a bit. It was only several blocks away and it was like being in your own little world. There were always mourning doves there that made the place sound eerie. We fished, swam, shot our guns and played with fire. One of our favorites was to shoot carp with a bow and arrow. We converted target arrows by putting a nail on the end that had been bent like a hook. We tied a long piece of fish line to the arrow so we could pull in the fish. I always carried my BB pistol when I went to the river. I shot at every target I could find. Swimming wasn't quite as nice as it sounds because the river was dirty. Every town along it's course dumped raw sewage into the river. We did play in the mud and then washed off in the river. I brought small jars of gasoline to the river and burned down the things I built from sticks. My friends had a seine so we would seine the ponds that were left when the spring water would recede. They were full of baby fish and we were amazed at how these tiny fish looked exactly like the big ones. I brought two painted turtles home from there and named them Myrtle and Christopher. They were about the size of a 50 cent piece. I put them in a serving tray and added some sand and water. I fed them flies that I swatted on the front porch. If the flies were still alive they would buzz in the water and the turtles would come down off the sand and swim out to the fly and chomp it down in one bite.

We went to Sibley Park quite often. Sometimes my

dad would drive us there but we also had access by bike so we went there with other kids. It was in a beautiful location near the river. The park had large grazing areas for buffalo (bison) and we thought they might be about the only ones left after reading our history books. They had a zoo there, also, with the usual animals found in a small zoo. They had a bear but it had to be put away because it killed the keeper. There was a dog in with the lion that seemed like an odd situation. They had a small alligator, or crocodile, that hardly moved so we used to get a big mouthful of water from the nearby drinking fountain and spit it on him. He seemed to like that.

There was a hill in the park and a museum at the top. There was an old car up there that seemed ancient but it was probably only about 40 years old.

There was a damn across the river that was built by the WPA (Work Projects Administration) and meant for recreational use. We used to fish there but not with bait. There was a spillway just under the falls where the carp used to hang out. We would use a daredevil and cast out and jerk the line to snag them. When a big carp was caught in the tail it would give a mighty struggle.

There was a baseball game at Tanley Field every Sunday afternoon. There were also games in the evening but not every week. North Mankato had a team that played in a league with the other towns in Minnesota of similar size like Austin and Albert Lea. They were semi-pro and had a mix of amateurs and low paid pros. I went to many games but seldom paid the admission. I shagged balls that went over the fence or waited until they stopped charging. There was a cheap section of bleacher seats out past third base. It might even have been free. Sometimes I sat out by the score board on top of the fence. The announcer would tell me to get down from there but I would usually just move a little. The announcer was one of the two barbers that cut my hair.

Toni, the popcorn man, would bring his popcorn wagon to the games and park it right outside the entrance. It was a part of the game. There was a water fountain there but no pop was sold. A fire started in his wagon one day when I was there. It got out of control in a hurry and the flames were licking at the wooden stands. The police got Toni out first (he was trying to round up his money and got burned pretty badly), then they attached the wagon to the back of the police car and pulled it safely away from the stands. The flames were 15 or 20 feet high by then. The volunteer fire department finally arrived and put out the fire before it destroyed the wagon completely.

There was a big park across the street from Tanley Field where I spent a lot of time. It had tennis courts, a football field, a band shell, and a free ice skating rink. There were a lot of trees that dropped their leaves in the fall. Some kids from our school used to play football against some of the kids from the Catholic school. I was in those games and was often the runner. Our huddle consisted of, "Give the ball to Clayt and go right." I remember saying, "Give it to someone else because I don't have my breath back from last time." Skip and I used to play tennis here even after dark. Her mother asked where she was going with the racket after dark. We said, "We could still see." I went to the free skating rink a few times but usually I went to the hockey rink where my friends were. After listening to a football game I would sometimes go to the park just to kick the football. If there were lots of leaves I could pretend to do flying tackles into a pile of leaves.

Listening to the radio now was even better because we listened to weekly shows like *Lux Radio Theater*, *The Little Theater off Times Square*, *Jack Benny*, *Fred Allen*, and *Red Skelton*. The comedy shows all had something they would repeat every week like Fibber's closet on *Fibber Magee and Molly*. Jack Benny would send Rochester to the vault or start his Maxwell. The sponsors had gimmicks to repeat also like '903 Red' for a new cigarette that Red Skelton was promoting for Raleigh. Music wasn't played on the radio very much and for a while only live programs were allowed to be aired because of an agreement with the musicians union.

We still listened to the University of Minnesota football games and sometimes heard the high school basketball play-off games. We didn't have a very good radio and it was hard to tell what was said. We would ask each other, "What did he say?" Sometimes we would lie on the floor with our heads underneath to hear it better and sometimes a stomp on the floor would cause the radio to get better.

I didn't read very much but I did go to the library to read *Popular Science*. An article about a 'fox hole' radio fascinated me. It was a radio that was used by the GIs to get local radio stations without much cost. Actually it was a crystal set but no crystal was needed. It used a razor blade and a safety pin with some pencil lead attached instead. It needed a coil and a wire antenna. It also required a headset but I had gotten one from Grandpa years before. I wasted no time putting one together and I was surprised the first time I could hear KYSM. I had my own radio.

There weren't any hills to ski near us so we spent most of our winter sporting on skates. We had a hard time giving it up completely so we asked Dad to drive us to a hill. We had a good time skiing the hills of the Minneopa Golf Course but not very often.

The town had a hockey team that played against other nearby towns. This team or club also ran the rink and warming house for the public. They charged a dime and played music from worn out 78 rpm records. The rink was right down near the river. I still didn't have a pair of skates that fit and I spent a lot of time sitting on the boards or in the warming house. The warming house was a nice place because that's where most of the kids were anyway.

We used to play Pump-Pump-Pull-Away as a game all could play. I got tripped once and went down hard and hit my head on the ice. I woke up in the back of the warming house where the 'club' members were playing cards. One of them looked over at me and asked if I was all right. I couldn't get up right away so they let me lie there for a while. When I did get up, one of them took my skates off and sent me on my way. I was suppose to peddle papers next but I told my substitute to peddle them. I started walking home but when I got to Belgrade Avenue I went into the office of the only cab company in town and asked to be driven home. When I got home, no one was there so I went up to bed and fell asleep. I slept through supper and my folks worried that I hadn't come home from the paper route but someone found me before too long and everything was fine.

Hayrides were popular and were often sponsored by a youth group at a church. Sometimes we would cross lines and go with a group from another church. The first time I went it was with Skip and her church group.

We never missed a High School football game even when it meant walking up the Main Street hill on a bitter cold night. I didn't have clothing warm enough to sit still in the stands for the whole game but we would run around and pretend to be playing football behind the stands. It helped to keep warm.

Art's Deluxe was a hamburger joint (this was a term of endearment) on the corner where Belgrade turned to go across the bridge. Everyone liked his hamburgers but they cost a lot of money and people didn't eat out very often. He put the buns on the grill with the hamburgers so they were warm and greasy. In the winter I used to stop in to get warm after walking across the bridge.

I wish I could say I ate there a lot but actually I remember wishing I had enough money to go in and order anything I wanted. Even when you didn't go in, the smell as you walked by made you wish for a hamburger.

Eighth Grade

We got all new teachers at the beginning of 8th grade. They were all good teachers but 8th grade was pretty much a repeat of 7th grade so it was too easy. This caused us to be bored with school subjects. This combined with our age made us incorrigible. I'm surprised the teachers put up with us. It helped that they were all first time teachers and had endless energy. Miss Hannah Lambert taught math and science. These were my favorite subjects but little was available to learn that year. Bill had already taught me the basics of algebra when I was in 6th grade, so the math of ?'s instead of x's and y's made little sense to me. When Bill got to 9th grade they taught him algebra and he liked it so much that I asked him what it was about. He told me the rules of equations and then showed me how to solve three equations and three unknowns. I had no idea how to set up the equations but I could solve them. When that got too easy he gave me one with y squared so there were two answers, plus and minus. There were students in class who were having trouble with math as it was taught so it had to be done. I'm just disappointed that there were no advanced classes available. Science classes have always been interesting but labs in 8th grade left something to be desired. The students had no equipment. The teacher set up the experiments in front of the class while we watched. One of the first experiments that Miss Lambert did was a disaster. She was showing us that water boiled at 212 degrees. She put a thermometer into a rubber stopper with a single hole. She then put the stopper in a Erlenmeyer flask half full of water. Next the flask was put on a ring stand over a Bunsen burner and we waited for the water to boil. I couldn't believe it. I turned to my buddies and their eyes were peeled waiting for the explosion. The thermometer went straight to the ceiling where it shattered. Thankfully, no one was hurt. Afterward she asked us to point out any future problems before they went that far.

Betty Morphew, who happened to be Skip's sister, taught English. She emphasized grammar rather than literature much to my liking. I wasn't a reader even if I had the time to do it. We had little time for homework so we just didn't do it. Even book reports were done without reading the books. She had a good sense of humor and I used to test it. Once she gave us a spelling assignment and said we should make a sentence using the 16 spelling words. Dick Ryan and I took her literally and put together one long sentence using all the words. She laughed and said that was good work but she would give us credit only if we diagrammed the sentence. We got down on the floor with a large piece of brown paper and began. With some help, we were able to do it. We had some bad times too. Once she wouldn't sign my permit slip that was required before each basketball game. She also gave me a C one quarter for something related to my conduct. I reacted by giving her the wrong answers to all her questions as if to say, "What do you expect from a C student?" I finished a test on diagramming early one day so I drew in a musical scale with notes and the word 'whistle' near the sentence that read, "*That is my sister playing the piano.*" I had nearly a perfect test but she took off 4 points because I had the treble clef sign backwards. She went skating with us occasionally after school. She would borrow Skip's skates and let me lace them up for her. She said, "You should be able to do that with all the practice you've had."

Ivan Underdahl was the other new teacher. He taught us social studies and was our coach. He was a very precise person in action and dress. He never said 'but'; he said, 'however'. When he took us to the park for recess, he explained the rules of touch football. We told him we only played tackle football. After some consideration he agreed and we were having a ball. One side was definitely better than the other, so he played with the weaker team even though he had on a three piece suit. This delighted the other side who made sure he ended up with grass stains on it. I ended up with a bloody nose so he told me to go to the sidelines and lie on my back. I had bloody noses before and knew that wasn't going to work. I tried but almost choked.

Walking to and from school in the spring was fun especially when there was rubber ice covering some water in the lot across from the park. When we stepped on the ice it would give but not break unless one stayed in one place too long. We wore overshoes but the water was deeper than that. We were more daring going home because it wasn't fun to have a wet foot in school all day. When we got to school there was a game going on that we could join anytime. It was like football and soccer together without rules. The idea was to get the ball across the other goal line by any method. Kicking, carrying, throwing all were acceptable. The Bohrer brothers, Harold and Rick, were always on opposite sides which was good because they were the only ones with enough courage to tackle the other. There was only one injury that I recall, which was a broken leg.

I volunteered to be a Patrol Boy because I knew I would get one free week at Camp Patterson. We stayed in cabins that slept about 12 or 15 kids in bunks. Each cabin had an older boy as a counselor. Ours was Jerry Aune. We spent a lot of time in the water and I passed Junior Lifesaving. This was a YMCA camp and one of the Mankato leaders came out to talk to us. He parked his car near the beach. Someone released the hand brake and the car rolled into the lake. The water was only a few inches deep but he was very unhappy.

I loved to play sports as did all the boys. I'm sure the girls would have also had they had the chance. I guess my best year was in 8th grade when I was the center on the basketball team and got a letter in track. I wish I could say I was really great in basketball but that's not the case. Luckily no one was so we enjoyed playing with others of the same ability. Ken Uhlhorn played one forward and Lloyd Horness played the other. The guards were 7th graders,

Duane Swan and Bob Kulseth. Our coach was Ivan Underdahl. We played several other junior high schools in Mankato and went to play in nearby towns, as well. Ken Uhlhorn's dad would drive some of us to the games. I think we won most of the games. I had a problem with my right heel, which was so sore I couldn't always wear a tennis shoe. I wore a regular shoe that had a gum rubber sole. The coach of Franklin, Melvin Mauseth, didn't want me to play with those shoes but Ivan talked him into letting me play.

Track was nothing but practice after school with one track meet per year in Mankato between all the junior highs. I tried lots of things but found I could be competitive only in the high jump and high hurdles. Dick Ryan ran the mile and I thought I could do anything he could do. I started out on the 1/4 mile track and went around once when I realized I wasn't going to make it 3 more times so I quit. I think my heel problem came from doing the scissors high jump into a pit with no sand. I had track shoes that made it worse because they have no cleats on the heel.

I got a chenille letter for lettering in more than one area. I had it put on the back of my best jacket and proudly wore it to 9th grade where the jacket was stolen the first week.

Track and basketball were the only organized sports in our school but we played everything else on an informal basis. We played baseball and softball in the park. We even played some tackle football but without any equipment it was pretty hard. There were tennis courts in the park and I played tennis sometimes. I also played golf in the park with a 7 iron and a couple of balls. Bowling was my favorite but that wasn't done with the same friends. I knew golf and bowling were sports I could play the rest of my life so I didn't mind that the team sports in school didn't pan out in the next few years.

Bill and I would play catch with a softball or baseball but I too often threw it wildly and he would have to go after it. He wasn't very patient about that. He usually pitched and I caught. He wanted to throw a curve so badly that he would ask, "Did it curve?" and I would say, "Yes," even though I never saw it curve.

I did hunt squirrels in the fall after the leaves fell. The .22 I used was my dad's and he said he won it on a punch board at the Elks Club. He taught me to shoot it on vacation at Mission Lake when I was very young. It had a telescopic sight so I could lie down and shoot at targets that he put up. He started with an old straw hat of his. I shot a few squirrels and justified it by telling myself they were just rats with bushy tails. I usually went with someone who would clean and eat them so I felt I was just helping them shoot them. It wasn't long before I didn't like to kill them either.

On one of the squirrel hunting trips in the woods north of town Dick Bjorgel brought a shotgun. It came in pretty handy because we had started a fire in a hollow tree to get a squirrel out but the fire got too big for us to control. Dick stepped up with his shotgun and blew the thin side of the tree away so it fell down. We were able to get to the fire with dirt and put it out.

I even went hunting deer with a bow and arrow that I made in the Scouts. Two of us waited by a place where we had seen deer coming for water in the evening. When they came I decided that each was too small, too big, or the other fellow would shoot it. He didn't.

Our school had a working bell, but for quite a few years, it was rung only at graduation. Somewhere along the line it was decided that the bell and cradle were too old for this and the practice was stopped. The night of our graduation we were told not to try because the janitor would be on guard all night so we didn't bother. It didn't mean that much to us anyway. The day after graduation we went to school around noon to get our report cards. As I was walking to my class I noticed the rope to the bell hanging by Mr. Dubke's office as usual and no teachers were around. I went over to it and gave a pull. Nothing seemed to happen, so I pulled a little harder and harder. Mr. Dubke was nearing the school when the bell started ringing. He hurried in and up the stairs in time to catch me. He grabbed me by the collar and pulled me into his office, which was right under the bell tower. He was giving me a good tongue lashing when a couple of teachers came to tell him that his public address system was turned on and his lecture was going to all the rooms. At that moment he just motioned for me to leave.

The Drug Store

The day I turned 14 years old I walked into the local drug store and asked for a job. The child labor laws were strictly enforced then. It was illegal to do certain kinds of work until you were 14 years old. The enforcers used to harass us constantly at the bowling alley. I knew there was a vacancy because Jim Taylor had just quit. He couldn't have worked there very long because he was in my class. Anyway I got the job starting out at 27 cents an hour. I was to work every day after school. Monday, Wednesday, and Friday I worked 4:00PM until 6:00PM. Tuesday and Thursday I would work 4:00PM to 5:00PM and then 6:00PM until closing. Closing was 10:00PM when I first started but changed to 8:00PM a year or so later. Tuesday was when we scrubbed the floor after closing. That usually took until 11:00PM. Saturday my hours varied, but usually I put in a full day. I then worked every other Sunday from 9:30AM to 1:00PM and 2:30PM to 6:00PM. The store was closed 1:00PM until 2:30PM. This totaled about 23 hours one week and 30 hours the next. I kept this job until the flood in 1951 that was 4 years later. When I quit I was making 60 cents an hour. Between school and the drug store there wasn't much time for other things. Every Wednesday I did find time for Boy Scout meetings. I also played basketball in 8th and 9th grades so I had to do a lot of trading of hours and there were times they just let me off.

Mr. Apple owned the store when I started and it was called Apple's Drug Store. He had a son, Bob, who worked there and taught me a lot of the things I was suppose to do. Bob was only 2 or 3 years older than I and was like a buddy.

The store was actually 2 stores side by side. One side was the drug store and the other was called a Gift and Soda Shop with a Post Office in the back. I spent most of the time at first in the Gift and Soda Shop. Gifts included quite a nice selection of cameras. Mr. Apple liked to sell cameras. His favorite sales pitch included some nude female transparencies that were shown through a little viewer. I borrowed a few and took them to Dick Ryan's house where we made them bigger with his enlarger. Then we went to John Kolling's house where we developed them. John's mother later found them and put him out of business for a while.

I had to cover for someone in the drug store every once in a while when they went home for lunch and I hated it because I didn't know where anything was. It wasn't like today where everyone finds his own goods, a clerk was asked to find everything. Even tooth paste and shaving soap had to be taken off the shelf by the clerk. I could find a few things like that but most requests were for things I had never heard of before.

There was a gal who worked there who's last name was Beetsch. She wasn't very tolerant of me and whenever I asked her where something was, she would say, "Up Mike's ass." Once I asked her for help and told her I had already checked Mike. She almost smiled and was quite a bit better after that. I couldn't complain about her because she was living with the owner. No one quite knew where his wife was and I never talked about it with Bob.

Bob and I used to scrub the floor together and sometimes we would put a 6 pack of beer in the ice cream freezer so we could have a reward when we got done. Once we decided we needed a reward before we started so we had one first and then another. When Bob decided we better get the scrubbing done, he stood up, stepped on the mop, held onto the handle too long and fell flat on his face. We didn't mop that night. Another time we got water in a floor electrical socket. It blew a fuse and the store went dark. I guess it dried by morning. If we weren't careful with the mops they would throw dirty water up on the glass cases and the gals would have to clean them the next day. We always heard about that.

Up until I was 15 years old, there was no test required for a driver's license. We sold them in the drug store for 35 cents. I can't remember what kind of identification was required but I sold them as part of my duties. The year I was old enough for a license, they required a driving test

Working as a Soda Jerk was fun. We had two booths and about 7 stools. We served a lunch menu with hot beef sandwiches and a cold plate. Most of my work was at the soda fountain with ice cream cones, floats, sodas, and even banana splits. We also had hand pack ice cream made from the 2 or 5 gallon ice cream cans. It was better ice cream and the price was right. Some time later we weighed some ice cream and calculated that it cost a nickel per scoop and it was sold for a nickel so the profit was not in the ice cream. We had the best root beer anywhere. We made the syrup right there. It was made from a gallon of sugar, 4 ounces of Park Davis' root beer extract and a gallon of boiling water.

Sundays were pretty busy and I barely had time to wash the dishes before they were needed again. People would come in bunches. They would come before church for coffee, after church for coffee, and after the movies for ice cream. One of the church crowd thought my coffee was so bad he volunteered to come early to make it. I thought that was fine and he did for a long time. There were quiet times, too, when no one was in the store. Sometimes during a rain storm, no one was out and we could relax and look out at the rain coming down and get paid for doing nothing.

A Close Call

Tornadoes were an expected event in the summer. We didn't have warning systems but you knew after a really hot muggy day, cool weather would eventually come and with it a tornado someplace. Many towns around Mankato were hit and we would read about it in the paper. I had only one really close call. Bill and I were playing golf at the Minneopa Golf Course. We had gotten a ride out there somehow and were playing the 8th hole, which was parallel to the highway. I've never known Bill to quit anything but that day he said, "Lets quit after 8 and hitch hike back to town." It was terribly hot and muggy but he hadn't said anything about it before. We finished the hole and went out onto the highway to hitch a ride. The first or second car picked us up with golf clubs and all. We got out at Front and Main so we could walk across the bridge to North Mankato. Before we got across the bridge, we heard sirens from ambulances and fire trucks going to the scene. It caught our attention because there were so many of them. In the time it took us to drive the 4 or 5 miles to town, the tornado had struck right where we were standing and the call had gone out for help. There was a Motel called The Green Gables right across the street from the spot where we had gotten the ride. It was leveled with the loss of many lives. The golf course was also leveled. The trees were all shredded but the main part of the tornado missed the clubhouse.

Ninth Grade

Graduating from 8th grade was sort of an end to a feeling that I was at the top of the heap and everything was there just for me to enjoy. Ninth grade was different. It was back to Franklin School, which was a couple of miles away from home and transportation was at a minimum. Walking was the usual way to get there and back. Franklin was used as a 9th grade junior high for everyone in town. Even the kids from the Lincoln school area were bused there. At least it felt good to be in the part of the building that had been just for the older kids when I was there in grade school. I was surprised that so many of my old classmates were not there. Some had gone to church schools and some had flunked a grade or two and were just waiting to get old enough to quit. I didn't get a new principal, however, because Mr. Vistad was now the Franklin Junior High Principal. I met some new friends and was especially interested in the girls. Harriet MacDonald, everyone called her Mac, was very friendly. I liked that but nothing ever came of it. I only saw her in the hall because the Lincoln kids had separate classes.

I liked Industrial Arts Class that consisted of a half a year of mechanical drawing and a half a year of woodworking. Mr. Beamer taught both of these subjects. He was quite a guy and had his own ways of maintaining discipline. If he caught you whistling, he would come up behind you and jab a sharp pencil in your rear. I saw him coming once and put my hand behind me just in time to get the pencil in my thumb right beside the nail. The lead broke off and stayed in my thumb. When I showed it to him he said, "I'll fix that". He took his pocketknife out of his pocket and took the lead out like he was coring an apple. That was his standard way of taking out slivers so no one went to him twice for that. I made a coffee table out of solid walnut. I still have it. The legs were turned on the lathe to a design that Bill had drawn. It was hard to get it done in time so other teachers used to let me out of their class early so I could spend extra time in the shop.

Miss Older taught the long awaited algebra class that I took. At first, I was excited about it but it turned out to be too much busy work and not much learning. I wanted to learn how to set up the equations rather than spending so much time solving them.

Miss Marshall taught business. I don't remember what the course was about but I liked her. She had an Oldsmobile that had an automatic transmission. She let me start it once to warm it up in the middle of a cold day. I couldn't believe it had no clutch. She also was in charge of a comedy sketch that we put on for the rest of the school. It was called a minstrel show. I think it was patterned after a vaudeville act. We blackened our faces and asked questions of the 'interlocutor', played by Dick Ryan. The answers were all canned jokes that had survived over the years. Mary Meyer was draped in a flag and stood to one side of the stage. I assume I have forgotten something significant about that.

I have forgotten the name of my English teacher but she was the one that sent to speech correction class not knowing about my braces. She loved poetry and spent a lot of time trying to teach us the iambic-pentameter stuff. She had a favorite poem that went, in part like this, "Poor Floyd Ferguson for his hard heart, tarred and feathered and carried in a cart by the women of Marblehead". She would try to make it all rhyme and would say, "Poor Floyd Forguson for his ord ort, tored and feathered and carried in a cort by the women of Marblehead."

I also sang in a choir. Mr. Hessla let me sing because there was a shortage of boys that were willing to try. I felt at home with him because I had taken some trombone lessons from him in 4th grade. Singing in the boy scouts was fun and many of the same guys were in the choir.

I went out for both football and basketball but wasn't good enough to start so it wasn't much fun. Football was all calisthenics except for the scrimmages that were played in a sand burr patch. I tried to play fullback but I wasn't built right to put my head down and run into the line the way I was told to do. One time I ran around end and gave Don Peterson a stiff arm (in self-defense). He went to the ground and I went for a touchdown. The coach (Merv

Woverton) chewed Don out something awful but never said a word to me. I knew then that the game wasn't for me. I quit the day the coach tackled me to show how it was suppose to be done. He hit me so hard it knocked my shoes off. I simply left my uniform on the floor by his door. I had better things to do. Nothing was ever said to me. Basketball wasn't much better but I was built better for it. I weighed 116 pounds at the time and was close to 6 ft. tall. I remember that because I tried to play on the small team but the weight cut off was at 115 pounds.

The coach was Melvin Mauseth. He was also my science teacher. He was a very cynical person and always had that little smirk on his face. In science I liked that because he intimidated all those that didn't know the answers to his questions. When someone would give him the wrong answer, he would say, "Clayton, what is the correct answer?" This way he could show that he had done his part in teaching the class but not everyone was listening. It also kept me alert. Ed Sorenson (Eggs) was my chief competition so Mr. Mauseth would play us against each other pretending to favor one over the other.

He asked me to come out for basketball but that was where his help ended. As a matter of fact I don't remember ever getting any coaching as such. Coaches in the lower grades were not paid much extra money to coach and often never played the game they were coaching themselves. They often read the rules and taught them to us and then just let us play. Mr. Mauseth let me start a few games but it only to punish Wayne Hoffman for something he had done wrong. I started one game at Loyola and got 4 fouls in the first quarter. They were all for the same thing. The referee called it "over the shoulder" but there was no such thing. After each call I complained and looked to the coach for help but he just looked at me with that silly smirk. I was taken out of the game so I went to the dressing room, put my clothes on and went home. I don't remember if I played again or not. Stan Cooper had just been kicked off the team for smoking and I thought I might be next. I was also having trouble getting that much time off at the drug store so I chose to give up on basketball. I still had bowling and golf and they didn't involve coaches or referees.

While we were in 9th grade, the high school kids walked out of school to protest the lack of a new high school building. It had been 5 years since the old one had burned and the city fathers were still bickering about where it should be located. When we got word of it we tried to leave school as well, but Mr. Vistad was waiting at the door and told us we weren't going anywhere.

If nothing else were happening I would go to the YMCA. It was quite a long way from home but I got my hair cut down stairs in their building so I had an excuse to hang around on the first floor where they had the pool tables. They were always busy and could be rented for 5 cents an hour. Actually there was one older table that was only 1 cent an hour. Sometimes I would go swimming in the pool there. One didn't have to plan ahead for this because swimming suits were not used. I never quite understood this and was given a variety of strange answers when I asked why they weren't used. The pool itself was nice but had a rather low ceiling so the diving board use was limited.

Learning to drive a car was one of the highlights of the year. I started with my dad's '38 DeSoto. First, I practiced with the clutch in our driveway. Next, Dad let me drive to the dump that was straight down the street a few blocks. On the second attempt I left the emergency brake on and burned it up. Dad was not happy and I was embarrassed. Bill let me drive his '37 Dodge a couple of times and Chuck Frost would let me drive his Pontiac over to the other store occasionally.

I was out to Masonic Beach with Jim Taylor once when he found a girl that agreed to come back with us in his car. His dad had a new Plymouth 5-passenger coupe and Jim got to use it often. Sometimes he used it without his dad's knowledge. I know that because I was with him when he took it. On this day he asked if I could drive because he had a chance to sit in the back seat with the girl on the trip to town. I said, "Sure". But I had never driven on the highway before. It seemed pretty easy until we got to town and Jim said, "Let's pull into the Drive Inn and get a root beer." I turned in but didn't slow up enough and we skidded all the way across their gravel parking lot. Luckily we didn't hit anything. He sat up in the back and said something derogatory but I pretended that I had done it on purpose.

Until that year anyone could get a driver's license as soon as they were old enough. Now we had to get a learner's permit and drive with a licensed driver until we took the driving test. The test was difficult and I had to take it twice. It included arm signals and parallel parking between flags. Arm signals were used to indicate turns and stops because we didn't have turn signals on the cars. They went like this: a left turn was signaled with the left arm straight out the window, a right turn was signaled with the arm bent at the elbow with the hand held straight up, and a stop was the same with the hand pointing straight down. Most cars had stoplights but some cars had only one small one. When it was really cold, my dad would open the left door to indicate a left turn. I don't know what the origin of this signal was but it sounds dangerous now especially since we had no seat belts.

High School

I looked forward to high school but in many ways it didn't live up to my expectations. The best part was the after school activities. Part of the problem was the school itself.

Recent Photo of Lincoln School

Lincoln School was built as a junior high and was being used as a high school. Not only that, but there were at least twice as many kids crowded in there than the building was intended to hold. We were given only 3 minutes between classes and the halls were jammed so one had to plan ahead. Getting to your locker, unlocking it, getting a different book, and getting to the next class using one way stairs was a challenge. Going to the bathroom was almost impossible during this time. The stairs were designated up and down because they couldn't handle all those kids going both ways. The boy's bathroom was near the up stairs and the girl's was near the down stairs. One had to know this because the signs, that said boys or girls, were screwed on over the door and could easily be swapped. This happened each year when the new sophomores would arrive.

The auditorium was used as a study hall. All students who had that hour free would go there. A plywood lap-board was available so a sort of table could be put on your lap to hold your book or help in writing. Sometimes they were used like frisbees and thrown at the stage. I spent just enough time there to know I was never going to study there so I took extra classes like choir or speech to have a place to go. We also ate lunch in the auditorium. There was a lunchroom but they sold food there and I never bought any.

I was a hall monitor for a while. There were two to each floor and we would check students for passes as they came by. We also swept the floor.

It was an awkward time for me. I grew to 6'4" somewhere during my high school days and gained hardly any weight. I often dressed poorly in a sort of defiant way and was self-conscious all the time. I did have one good friend through a lot of this time who didn't seem to mind. His name was Jimmy Nielsen. We were known as Mutt and Jeff because he was short. He had a car and a father that paid for the gas. His dad owned the Lincoln–Mercury garage in town and had a model A all fixed up for him. We went everywhere together and shared many of the same feelings about school. The first time I saw him I was at the YMCA.

Clayt and Jimmy, circa. 1952

At time the upstairs of the YMCA was called "the Attic" and it was a nice place to go to see others your age.

I was outside with some friends when he came around the corner in his model A. He was going too fast and the car was nearly on two wheels. I said, "Who is that crazy nut?" It was Jimmy. It was a while before we met but we seemed to hit it off right away. I met many new kids from the other the parts of town. Some were to become good friends, like Dick Randall. His dad owned the Hamm's Beer Distributing franchise in Mankato. Dick helped his dad and the drivers load and unload beer trucks. There was always plenty of cold beer in the walk-in cooler so I hung around and helped load trucks whenever I could. We were suppose to pay 15 cents for a bottle, but I usually just stuck a finger into the coffee can and stirred the change so it sounded like I was paying. I did that in church as well. Dick's dad let him drive the pickup truck as soon as he got a license.

He also had a Harley Davidson motorcycle. I forgot the number associated with it but it was the big one. I rode on the back of that bike many times. It went 115 mph that I know of but probably could go faster. It couldn't be stopped very easily, however, when it was going that fast. We had to go into the ditch once when two milk trucks were blocking the road so they could talk. We saw the trouble a long way back but still we were going about 50 mph (I looked at the speedometer) when we went in the ditch. Dick knew how to ride so we didn't spill.

His folks had a cabin at Lake Washington and a fine speedboat.

Dick's dad was a Shriner so we had access to the Masonic Beach swimming area at Lake Washington. It was a better beach than the public ones, like Squirrel's Nest.

My attendance record in school was terrible, mostly because school started so early in the morning. I had to catch a bus shortly after 7 in the morning and that was hard for me to do. Sometimes I would hear the bus go by when I was still in bed and dress in a couple of minutes and run 2 blocks to where the bus came down Belgrade on it's way to school. Staying at home was no fun either. Mother would turn the radio to soap operas that I hated and even Arthur Godfrey was so boring that I would rather have been in school.

It wasn't an easy thing to skip that much school. We had an attendance officer, Mr. Vick, who would toss the pink pad at me when I would show up at his window. He had a little booth out in front the Principal's office like he was selling tickets to the theater. The pink pad meant unexcused absence with the time to be made up in 'detention'. The only thing he couldn't argue about was sickness, so I would go into the nurse's office and tell her how sick I had been. Her name was Miss Billet and she favored boys. She was very sympathetic and always gave me a good checkout before giving me the blue ticket back to class.

My report cards (I still have a couple) reflected this poor attendance and the grades were usually about a B. I liked math and science but nothing else. I never did homework because there was no time for it. I carried a notebook and some books back and forth but never got to them. Some teachers gave us time at the end of class to get started on our homework and I could usually finish in that time. Other teachers expected us to read volumes of history or English and that never got done. I tried to read history in school but by the time I got to the bottom of a page, I couldn't remember what was at the top of it. I think I might have been interested if a different kind of history was taught but not the subjects they covered. Who cares about old English history when you are in high school in a different country?

Polio took its toll even among high school age kids. I remember two in particular. One was Shirley Robertson. She was two years older and came back from The Sister Kenny Polio Center on crutches. Dave Eilenfeldt was less lucky; he came back a year later in a wheel chair. He was a year older so he finished his last year with us. The stairs were no problem, however, he would just roll up to them and the next two boys that came by would carry the chair up the stairs. He had been a popular football star and I remember the two guys carrying him into the school one evening for a dance or something before anyone knew he had polio. The next day he was taken to Sister Kenny.

Donna Norlund sat right behind me in study hall the first year. I used to turn around and talk to her because she had such a pretty face. She also had a nice personality. She was probably 5 ft. even and I liked the short girls best. I don't remember how it came about but I took her on a hayride in the middle of the winter. My dad let me borrow the car and I went to pick her up. I hadn't been to her house before but I knew which one it was. She lived along the highway southwest of town toward Minneopa. There was a lot of snow on the ground and the ditches were full. I assumed that they had a driveway out to the highway so I turned in where it should be. There was no driveway so I went into the ditch. I didn't hurt the car and her dad pulled me out with some big equipment that was parked next door. He drove this equipment as part of his work. He told me I wasn't the first to drive into his ditch but I was embarrassed anyway. When we got to the farm where the hayride took place we all parked on the road. The plow had made the road look wider than it was by pushing the snow out a ways over the ditch. Luckily I avoided trouble this time but many other cars had to be pulled out of the ditch by the farmer after the hayride. I went out with her a couple of other times, once we went to an out of town basketball game. We went on the bus and had a good time. I can't remember the game but I remember the bus ride because cold air was coming in the window and I was trying to keep her warm. I can't remember why I stopped seeing her. It was just one of the many things I did then that made no sense.

Girls in general were of interest to me. The older girls were all pretty nice to me but I didn't get serious about them because they seemed so much older and more mature. The younger girls were also nice to my friends and me. They sort of looked up to us and there were a lot of good-looking girls in the two classes behind ours. I didn't get serious about them either. A couple of times girls asked me to go out and I went but I was never very nice to them. I took Harriet MacDonald to one of the school dances but I couldn't dance. She was all dressed up and we sat watching everyone else dancing. There wasn't even an event afterwards like there often was so the night was a disaster. I felt sorry for her. When I was with someone I really liked, I felt self-conscience so there are no interesting stories to tell about girls in high school. There were a few couples that went together the whole time and seemed destined to get married but usually it didn't last.

. Everyone had to take physical education but it was not anything to look forward to doing. There was a lot of running, some games and a shower. It was probably the shower that was considered most important. In the winter we would run around the perimeter of the gym and run up the stairs to the balcony, across the end of the balcony and down the stairs. This would go on forever, it seemed, so I would hide halfway up the stairs. I would wait for everyone else to make a complete circle so I could join them again. I played in the Saturday morning basketball league and enjoyed it so I wasn't against exercise.

Teachers

Mr. Lyle Roberts was my history teacher. He had the same routine everyday. He would give us a chapter of the book to read as homework and answer the questions at the end of the chapter. The next day we would go through the questions for an hour and then turn in our homework sheets. I would, of course, fill out a homework sheet as we were going through the answers. He would stand in the same place every day and put his foot up on the radiator. It was right next to me. He would watch me fill in the answers and tell the class that we weren't allowed to do that. He really was a nice guy and used to stop in our drug store everyday for a pack of Old Golds. Many times he would say to me, "I don't recall seeing you in school today." I would tell him that I didn't feel very good this morning but I was all right now. He never said anything to our attendance officer, Mr. Vick.

Miss Beth Bishop was one of my favorite teachers. She taught geometry and I loved it. Each year there was a student teacher day and she let me teach the class. She didn't even stay in the room after she determined that I was doing all right. She was also a popular advisor for student teachers from the local colleges. We had one that had been the homecoming queen at Gustavus. If we needed help with our homework, she would sit with us in those little seats so I would raise my hand for help even though I didn't need it. I'm sure Miss Bishop knew what I was doing but said nothing.

She came to my aid once later when I got into trouble with the student counsel's disciplinary board. She was the advisor to the student council so I went to her and told her I wasn't going to go to detention just because they had handed me a few hours for something trivial. I told her I didn't think they even had the authority to do it. She simply said, "OK." I didn't go and nothing was said about it. Donna Norlund was the chairman of this group but this episode had nothing to do with me not seeing her again but she probably thought so.

I took three years of English but no grammar was taught, so I wasn't interested. I can't remember learning anything. I remember the first day with Miss Joyce. I walked out just as she was ready to start class. She came after me and asked me what I was doing. I told her I didn't have a pencil so I was on my way to my locker to get one. She let me know that she didn't allow kids to leave her class whenever they wanted. I knew all that but I felt I had to establish the limits. She was called the 'little colonel' and deservedly so.

I took a year of chemistry from Karl Aaberg. I liked all science but there was too much memorization in his class, so I didn't do well. He didn't teach any of the logic of chemistry that makes it possible to predict reactions and reaction rates.

Miss Pinney was a student counselor but she never counseled me, or any one else, that I know of. We had to get her permission to change or add classes so I went to her to get permission to take speech instead of English in my senior year. She made me take both.

I took art one semester but no talent appeared there so I took a semester of typing. I am glad today for that introduction but I probably should have had a full year of it. Chuck Ingham sat next to me and made things interesting. He made too many mistakes in one of the speed tests so he dropped his typewriter onto the floor. I think that ended his typing career.

Mr. Krisinski was the principal but was not in charge of discipline. I don't know what he did but it must have been with the teachers because he had nothing to do with the kids. The only time we saw him was when he would introduce someone at assembly and afterwards would give us a sweeping wave with two fingers that meant the assemble was over and we should return to class. Sometimes I would be in class without a pencil and would be sent to his office where he would sell me one for a nickel.

I liked Eleonor Biebl who taught algebra and trigonometry. We called her Miss Biebl but sometimes I would say something to Elinor Holmberg. She was in our class so I would say, "Elinor" out loud to watch Miss Biebl's reaction. When she looked shocked, I would point to Elinor Holmberg and say I was talking to her. She knew I was toying with her because she had a hard time getting mad. She had a paperweight made in the shape of a turtle.

She was fond of it so I used to put it up on the molding that ran around the room at about 8 feet. The first time she missed it she asked if we had seen it so I pointed it out. I gave it back that time but would put it back whenever we wanted to protest something. I used to move it each day so it would slowly make it's way around the room. By now she just watched it's progress and when it went all the way around I would put it back on her desk. She was a good teacher and used to help me understand the chemistry equations that were set up by Mr. Aaberg. He would tell us to put the 'y' above the element and the 'x' below the grams or some such scheme that he had learned to set up the equations that were suppose to determine how much of one chemical would react with another chemical. Miss Biebl would say, "I think he is trying to say," and then she would make complete sense out of the problem. She had a 6 ft. slide rule that hung on the front wall over the chalk board. We took it down and hid it behind the radiator. She noticed it was gone and thought we had thrown it out the window because she was out in the hall when it came down. She looked outside but didn't see it. She probably looked out there first because we used to thrown the chalk erasers out the window. I can't remember how this ended but I think it was held to the wall with scotch tape and it eventually came crashing to the floor.

Sometimes I felt that she would have liked to be something other than a teacher but unmarried women with an education had very little choice on making a living.

I liked physics even though it was taught with very little enthusiasm. Mr. Christian Arnold taught from slides that were prepared by some professional organization. We had to have a small flashlight (which I still have) in our notebook because it was too dark in the room to take notes. The class was taught in the chemistry room so we sat on stools. No modern physics was taught. It was all Newtonian physics even though relativity showed that it was wrong 40 or more years earlier. He did teach me one thing that stuck with me. He said Physics was the heart of science and it was the pursuit of the truth. He went on to explain that the truth in physics lasted only until someone showed that it was wrong. This was unlike organized religion where the truth was dictated by a leader and no one was allowed to challenge it.

I would have liked to take shop but Mr. Ling had no discipline in there and I was told if you were making something really good someone would destroy it and no one was ever punished for it. He would lock the door to the shop each noon but many times one of his pupils would put a pencil in the key hole and break it off so he had to dig the pencil out with a pocket knife before the afternoon class could start. I was told that so many kids would sneak out the windows (shop was on the first floor), that he had nailed all the windows shut.

I took choir instead. It met everyday for an hour downstairs in the band room. I probably would have taken band but I couldn't play an instrument. Mr. Hesla taught choir. He was the same teacher I had in 4th grade for trombone lessons and 9th grade choir. We had to pass a test by singing for him but I think all the boys were admitted just as they were in 9th grade. I started out as a tenor my sophomore year and ended up singing 2nd base when I was a senior. I don't think my voice changed that much but I could do less harm that way. I always had to stand close to someone who knew the tune so I could follow their singing. As a tenor it was Lucille Joyce. I could learn the part after a while but I couldn't read much music. The tenor part was hardest. I wanted to sing the melody but that's not what tenors do.

The Minneapolis Symphony came to town and Mr. Hesla encouraged us to go to the performance. The next day he was asking us how we liked it and I told him that I would have liked it better if they had played some popular music. He replied, "Shut your mouth, your brains are showing". Evidently he was unaware of the success of the Boston Pops, but then so was I.

We did sing a lot of heavy music mostly church type. Some of it was even in Latin.

I liked Christmas time because we sang so many songs that I knew. We sang at Brett's, some old folk's homes and at the other schools in town. We would walk the halls and sing carols. I had to leave in the middle of walking our high school halls to go to work and Audre Rome stopped me and asked if she could borrow the robe and take my place. She wasn't in the choir but wanted to sing with us that day so I gave her my robe. We went on several trips on the bus to other towns to join other choirs in a sort of massive choir. St. Olaf would sponsor one of these each year.

After School

A year or so after I went to work at the drug store, Mr. Apple sold the store to John Thro who already owned a drug store in Mankato. We became Thro's North Mankato Drug, which was quite a mouthful when answering the phone. The name wasn't the only change that was to come. We got a new boss by the name of Ray Gauthier who was known as 'Babe' by his friends. He wasn't a pharmacist but had worked in another drug store for some time and knew his way around the drugs. He helped fill prescriptions and even did some himself. Most of the time Mr. Wyland was there and later Chuck Frost came and they were registered pharmacists. I got along fine with both Chuck and Ray. They both had spent time in B-17's during the war. Ray as a bombardier in the 8th Air Force and Chuck as a pilot. Chuck was a pilot instructor who started out in B 25's. Even John Thro was a pilot in the Navy and used to fly around town in a Stearman. They didn't talk about it much. Ray was a good teacher. He had only one motto and that was 'Get the money'. Almost all of the products came in several sizes so I used to ask, "What size?", when a customer would ask for something. He taught me to give them the biggest one without asking. If they wanted a smaller one; fine, let them say so. Ray liked a good cigar and took personal charge of the cigar case. He made sure that the humidifier was always wet. I smoked quite a few cigars myself but I stuck to the cheap ones like the 6-cent Headline. I was going to quit one summer for a better paying outdoor job but when I told Ray he sat down with me on the curb and told me I should stay. I did stay because he made me feel needed.

One year he let me take a box full of supplies that I thought I could sell at scout camp. It included such things as tooth paste, sunburn treatment, gum, and aspirin. I sold a few things but it wasn't worth the effort.

Years later I appreciated Ray Gauthier more because I had to work for some bosses that had absolutely no substance to their character.

John Thro gradually got rid of the gifts and started to combine the two stores into one. The two booths went, as did the lunch menu. I was spending more time clerking the regular drugs and the move helped me know where things were. Chuck let me use his car to get things from their Mankato store. He asked if I could drive and I said, "Yes," but I had never driven in town. I had trouble getting the pharmacists at the other store to help me. They were always busy and didn't want to stop what they were doing. There was one that was 'married' to the store. I was told they couldn't even get him to take a vacation. His name was Hellman and everyone called him Dutch. He was very anti-social and never talked to anyone. It is said that when Aureomycin first came out it was $1 per capsule. He filled a prescription for 40 of them and without any warning to the customer said, "That will be $40." Well, in those days you could rent a nice house for a month for $40. One day I called him Mr. Hellman and he dropped what he was doing to help me. I always went to him after that.

The Post Office was a North Mankato branch of the

Mankato Post Office. Gerry Purrier worked with me as a clerk and her grandmother ran the Post Office. When her grandmother was off everyone had to fill in so I had to learn how to run this as well. It was mostly weighing packages and looking up the cost. I almost lost my job over this once when Senator Val Imm came in to send his numerous weekly packages. He published a weekly paper and would mail bunches of them around the state. I said in all innocence that he had a lot of packages. He took that to mean we didn't want him to use this branch office. To tell the truth, I hated to see him coming and couldn't figure why he didn't use the main Post Office in Mankato where he lived and worked. Anyway he complained about me and wanted me fired. This was really an attempt to get even with me for not giving his son my paper route when I moved to North Mankato. I was told that if I called him (in the presence of my boss) and apologized, I could keep my job. I did this but felt it was an injustice. I don't think he came with his packages much after that. The Post Office was moved out of the rear of the Gift and Soda Shop over to the old drug store but we had nothing to do with running it after that.

One of my favorite jobs was window decorating. It changed with the season and I used to look at other windows in Mankato to get ideas for ours. Going back to school was always fun with the spiraling tablets and boxes of crayons. Christmas was a fun time with people buying perfumes and colognes that Ray said were the big sellers. Every year we brought out an expensive highly decorated mechanical toy that never sold.

Every once in a while there would be a big promotion going on like the ball point pen demonstration. Once it was a mechanical device that held a pen that would go around in circles on paper as the paper was slowly pulled through. The paper was allowed to form a big pile and would show how long the pen would write. Another time there was a big sales pitch for Hadacol cough medicine We sold so much we had an extra table in the front of the store just for it. I asked why it was so popular and was told that it was almost all alcohol but wasn't taxed; so it was cheap. Before that Lydia Pinkum was sold to many women for just the same reason.

The money in the tills was counted each evening to see how close it came to the register's numbers. It never matched exactly but was usually pretty close. I never did the counting but was often there when it was done and it seemed to produce some sort of excitement to see if we were 'ahead' or 'behind'. The tills or cash registers themselves were interesting. They would bring quite a bit today in an antique store. The big one had a full key board for everything including a clerk's identification letter. It was opened with a hand crank and produced a written record of each transaction on a roll of paper.

Many people had charge accounts and they were all kept by hand in a large file cabinet with each account separate. The charge slips were held in place by a spring. The managers never talked about these charge accounts but I'll bet there was a lot of money outstanding and I don't think they ever pressed anyone to pay up.

When Ken Uhlhorn came to work there he and I would alternate Sundays. He usually worked with Chuck and I worked with Ray. I was already friends with Ken from Scouts and basketball. We worked together after school and did a lot of trading of schedules so we could do the other things we wanted to do. We were together one Saturday night when it was his turn to work Sunday. We were out at Wollam's turkey ranch and found some watermelons to eat. We also had a bottle of wine so we drank the wine out of a half of a watermelon. Ken got pretty drunk and bent or broke his glasses. I was in no hurry to get up the next day but I finally went to the store to see how he was doing. When I got there he just finished waiting on a customer and he ran out the back door. I asked Chuck if he was all right and he told me he was a pretty sick kid. I told Ken to go home and I would finish for him. Of course, Ken would have to take the next two Sundays.

Rats were a problem the whole time I was there. I'm told all river towns have the same problem. Our store was more than a block from the river but that didn't help. The rats knew how to burrow down by the building and scratch through the soft limestone foundation to the basement. There was a bakery on one side and a delicatessen on the other so they were attracted in big numbers. They weren't bashful either, I could see them behind the ice cream cooler quite often. At night they would eat anything that was left out. We kept all pastries behind glass and we would put the ice-cream cones on top of the glass showcase where the rats couldn't get at them. If we forgot, they would eat the cones off even with the box from which they hung. We would have to wipe off the counter tops and the ice cream coolers first thing in the morning because the little footprints were visible on the black shiny tops. The basement was a scary place because of them. When we closed up at night we would turn off the lights starting in the area farthest from the stairs and working our way to the stairs. The last light had a long string on it so we could be half way up the stairs before we turned it off. Then we would close the cellar door, but that didn't keep them in the basement. I set traps in the basement and sometimes on the main level. This was done when I closed Saturday night and opened Sunday morning. One Sunday morning when we opened there were people waiting to come in and a rat had dragged a trap right out in the middle of the floor before he died. I brought in the Sunday papers and dropped the bundle right on the rat so no one would see him. Several people who bought papers wondered why they were in the middle of the floor.

Later, John Thro lent us his store cat who kept rats out of his other store in Mankato. First the cat got pregnant and then went on a killing spree. She would kill rats and put them in a pile for me to shovel up and put in a box for the trash remover. We thought that was fine but when the cat was due to have the kittens, she disappeared and we never saw her again. We thought the rats got her.

One Sunday morning the 'before church crowd' was seated on the stools having coffee when all of a sudden they left without drinking their coffee. Ray thought that was strange but when the same thing happened after church, we began to check into it and found a terrible odor seemed to appear by the stools periodically. We suspected a dead rat but couldn't find it because the smell would come and go. Finally we found it just behind the fan on the ice cream cooler. When the fan would come on it would blow the odor right across the stools. No wonder they left but no one ever mentioned it.

The 'new' store was very compact and easy to clerk. I still made mistakes, however. Once I gave a lady a glass of water when she asked for waterglass. Waterglass is sodium silicate and is used to preserve eggs.

We didn't use bags for the products that were bought; instead they were wrapped in paper and tied with string. It became a challenge to make a neat looking package out of the various shaped things. We also wrapped the sanitary napkins in paper so the customers could pretend they were carrying something else. This wrapping was a big job and we took turns doing it. I wanted to use Scotch Tape but Ray said it cost too much so I had to use the string.

One of the perks of working there was the peanut case. Hardly a day went by without my reaching in to get a few warm nuts or cashews. I also made malted milks and drank them, especially on scrubbing night. I did this to gain weight but it never helped. I also had a supply of cigarettes and had the money to buy them. We also sold liquor and Ray told me to lay money on the register if I wanted to buy some liquor. He didn't want me in that till because the laws on selling by a minor were as severe as buying by a minor. Sometimes I would put money on the till for a half-pint and sometimes I would forget. The half-pints were needed only for special occasions like New Year's Eve.

One of my chores was to bottle mineral oil. It was purchased in a 55 gallon drum and I would put the oil in pint and quart bottles. I had to be very careful so it wouldn't fill over the top because it was so hard to clean off the bottles. Then I would lick labels and put them on. The labels came in two colors. Pink ones that said 'non fattening' and blue ones that did not. The blue pints were 29 cents and the pink pints were 39 cents. They came from the same barrel.

Selling condoms in those days was done with great secrecy. They were kept in a drawer in the back by the pharmacists and there were little brown bags to put them in before you shut the drawer. Mrs. Vera Buckley worked there full time and was afraid to sell them. She would get me to wait on people that looked like they were going to buy them. She was often right because people buying them would avoid the female clerks. I had one embarrassing experience with them. A bowling friend of my dad's came in and asked me for a tin, I thought. When I came back with a tin of three, he poured it out of the bag in front of other customers and said, "What is this?" I said, "You asked for a tin, didn't you?" He said, "No, I asked for a ten." He just wanted to cash a check for $10. He blamed Chuck and said, "You put him up to that, didn't you." I just smiled.

I worked with a young gal for a while the last year I was there and if I asked about any of the female products, she would say, "I'll show you." She was a real tease. Her favorite trick was to squeeze behind me while I was operating the big cash register. There wasn't room if the drawer was out so she would say excuse me and proceed but just as she would get behind me she would give me a goose. Even when I knew it was coming it was hard to remain poised for the customer. I did get even. She was in the basement getting the bottom row of Kotex boxes out of a case. She was bent way over when I came by. When I got even, she almost jumped into the case. One day she was no longer working there and I wasn't told why she left.

Her husband sold Dad a 1949 Ford. It was a demonstrator and he gave Dad a good deal. The problem was that it was a 6 cylinder and Dad thought it was a V-8. It wouldn't start when it got cold and was hard to steer driving down the highway. Dad soon got rid of it in favor of a 1950 Buick. The Buick was quite a car. When he ordered it he got gunmetal gray because he thought that was appropriate for his position at Standard Oil. He also told the salesman that he would buy it if it came with Atlas tires that were sold by Standard Oil. The salesman didn't catch on right away and told him what kind of tires they came with. When he caught on, he arranged to get a set of Atlas tires from a Standard Station.

The Attic was a place to meet others and do things together. We didn't have to plan ahead we just went to the Attic. There was a place to dance but I didn't dance so I just watched and talked to others. On summer days the windows were open so we could sit out on the fire escape.

Mrs. Adams was in charge and the kids always behaved well there. She sold ice cream cones and sundaes. She also had a student helper. I think it was Georgia Enfield most of the time. I don't know what we would have done without it. I went there every night that something else wasn't happening and so did most of my friends.

At some point Jimmy's dad fixed up a 1937 Ford and gave it to him to replace the Model A. I don't remember anything being wrong with the Model A but the newer car was much better in many ways. It didn't have any better brakes, however, as the fender dents would soon demonstrate. I was with him on a couple occasions when a fender was creamed because we couldn't stop. He would give me a ride to the drug store in it after school. This was very nice because I don't think there was a bus to take us back to North Mankato after school. It was a long walk and especially bad in the winter because we didn't dress for the cold. It wouldn't be stylish. It was on one of these occasions that I got a part in the senior class play. Jimmy was going to give me a ride to work but he wanted to read for a part in the senior class play first so I said I would wait for him. We had lots of time because school was over at 3:20 and I didn't have to be at work until 4:00. I had no desire to be in the class play but when I showed up to meet Jimmy, Miss Melhouse asked me to read for a part. She knew me because I was taking Speech from her at the time. I did a poor job of reading but her mind was made up. I looked the part. So I was in the play and Jimmy didn't get his part. I thought that was unfair. The play wasn't very good but we went through it several times. We even went to the other schools in town to give some excerpts from it to stir up some interest hoping someone would come to the performances. Miss Melhouse asked me to give the introductions but gave me no help doing it, so I tried to make it humorous. I thought the play was pretty dull so I tried to give the impression that we were saving the funny stuff for the performances. I started out with the traditional, "LADIES AND GENTLEMEN" but I added, "AND MEMBERS OF THE FACULTY". The kids got a big bang out of that but one of the teachers at Franklin came over to me and asked why I didn't think they were ladies and gentlemen. I couldn't believe it. She probably enjoyed the play. During one of the performances, Mr. Fitterer told me to liven it up a little bit because it was dying. I added a couple of things that weren't in the script and got big laughs. The play was called, *The Bishop's Mantle* and I played the part of a janitor in the rectory. I had to look up the name in my old annual.

I don't remember when I first met John Baker but I know it was he who was driving the car the night the 'older classmen' cut off my hair. I saw him light a whole row of firecrackers in someone's locker one day. He beat a hasty retreat, but I waited to see the action. When the firecrackers started to go off, the locker door swung wildly open and closed. Smoke poured out and everyone came running to see what it was. John Larson, my homeroom teacher, wasn't very far away so he came around the corner in a hurry. Nothing else happened. John didn't get caught and I never asked why he did it. He was a nut for old cars. He bought, sold, and traded them usually getting the better of the deal. He claimed to have had 13 different Fords while still in high school. He bought a 1940 Ford that had been burned inside. I didn't see it before he started fixing it up but I remember him painting the dash and doorframes with wrinkle varnish. It really looked good. When he was about done, he brought it to the Attic where we were all looking at it. He said he got everything looking good but he couldn't get the burned smell out of it. I said, "Maybe if we smoke a few cigars in there, the cigar smell will replace the burned car smell". Three, or more of us got in and lit cigars. We stayed there as long as we could before we got out and shut the doors. The cigar smell stayed but now the car smelled both of cigars and of burned car. We worked a lot of jobs together later and became good friends.

Jimmy often came back to the Drug store at quitting time so we would ride around town or drive to someone's house to visit. There were some places like Dori Nelson's where we felt we could just stop in for a while. We also would go to Karene Michel's house. She was in our class and had a younger sister, named Nadene. Jimmy had sort of a crush on her so we would sometimes drive out to their farm. They raised steers so I asked what that was. I knew only about cows and bulls. When I was told I was shocked. I don't know if Jimmy and Nadene ever dated but it seemed fun to just stop in unexpectedly. I was suppose to keep Karene busy so Jim could be with Nadene. Somehow it never worked out but it was something to do.

Drive-ins were popular places to go when you had a car. We would drive around town and stop at the Drive-ins because there were other kids there and the owners didn't seem to mind if you stayed for a long time. It looked busy and there were always plenty of places to park. The owners hired the good-looking girls to wait on the cars (car hopping) so that was another incentive to hang out there. We did buy some food there too, but not often. I remember the hamburgers at the A & W were not made from patties but were made from a type of sloppy Joe mix and were very good.

One New Year's Eve, Jimmy and I went in his '37 Ford to a spot where I had hidden a small bottle of whiskey. I had buried it in snow that the plow had heaped up against a telephone pole. It was bitter cold and we would dig for a while with our hands and then run to the car to get our hand warm by a small gasoline driven heater. After searching for quite a while, I suggested that we go to my house and get a shovel. When we came back we counted telephone poles again and determined that we had been digging at the wrong pole. I took one poke with the shovel and heard a clink. I had hit the bottle. We very carefully uncovered it with our hands and found only the top had been sheared off. I held it upright while he drove back to my house where we poured the whiskey through a hanky into a fruit jar to strain out any broken glass. After that we went to the party.

We didn't often have whiskey because we could buy beer at a little grocery store called Landwier's. There was hardly anyone in the store and the owner would ask for identification but when you told him you didn't have any, he would give you a tablet of paper that said, "I swear I am 21 years old." We would sign someone's name, often it was Russell Pitz. It was kind of a local joke but I heard later there was a kid by that name. Jimmy wouldn't park out in front in case I got into trouble but when I showed up with the beer, he would drive up and pick me up. A six pack was plenty for the two of us.

In the spring of the year the basketball tournaments were played and Mankato usually did well because they were the only 'big' city in their district. Sometimes the 'little town' of Mountain Lake would beat them but we often went to the State Tournament in the Twin Cities. For those of us that didn't play, it was an excuse to get away from home and party for three days. Some kids had cars but most of us got around on the streetcars. We never saw a map of Minneapolis but somehow got around without one. We went in groups and someone in the group would know what streetcar to take. The games were played in the University's Field House. It was almost to St. Paul on Washington Avenue. We stayed in downtown Minneapolis so that was a long way. I didn't want to spend money on a room, so I would put a sleeping bag in a suitcase and sleep on the floor of someone else's room. One year we stayed in the YMCA. I brought some condoms from the drug store and we blew some up and sailed them out the window. We also filled some with water and dropped them onto the sidewalk. Once we hit the roof of a car and it put a dent in it. As we watched in horror, the dent popped out but the condom stayed there. We all drank and pretended to be drunk. We went to the Alvin to see the strip tease show. As we came out once, we ran into a bunch of girls from our school. They asked us what were we doing in a place like that. There was some minor damage done to the hotels but nothing that got anyone in trouble. I don't know how many games we won but it seemed important at the time.

Scout Camp

By now I was better prepared for scout camp. I even had a sleeping bag with an air mattress. We had a week-long camp each year and two or three camps of three days or less. Some were with other troops and called camporees. We had to rely on parents or other adults to drive us to camp but most of the time we were on our own after we got there. The week-long camp was at a lake so we got all the water sports along with the regular scout activities. Our troop had a kitchen fly (tent) where we could do our own cooking, but sometimes we ate at the lodge.

When we did our own cooking we had to buy the

supplies. We had a list of essentials but we always added things like cookies on our own. We often kept them locked up so only the few with keys had access to them. We supplied our own eating utensils and did our own dishwashing, if you could call it that. We usually put our dishes in a cloth netting and dunked them into a 55 gallon barrel of hot water.

We slept two to a tent and one of the first years I was paired with Franklin Delano 'Fat' Haake. He brought a quart of his mother's homemade wine so we drank it -- all at once. I got drunk but he said he didn't like it so I drank most of his, too. I was dizzy all night and sick the next day, especially when I drank a lot of water thinking it would dilute it. The next day was a Sunday and we were all hustled off to the outdoor church of our choice. I went with someone I knew but he went to a Catholic service and so did I. I just prayed that I wouldn't throw up.

We always initiated the first year campers. We would tell them to bring their bedrolls and be prepared to spend the night in the woods. They would bring as much as they could carry. Next, we blindfolded them and gave them a position along a long rope. We pulled the rope in and out of the woods for about a half an hour. When we took them off the rope, we would tell them to make camp right there so we could find them in the morning. We told them to keep their blindfolds on until we were all gone. Of course, when they took off their blindfolds they would find themselves right beside their tent.

Later, I chose to have John Kolling as my tent mate. Together we built a wooden box and filled it with all the little things that made our stay more comfortable. We would also check out a tent and repair and waterproof it beforehand. There still were no floors in the tents but by then we had our own army cots. We had Flit that we used to spray spiders. We would keep the tent closed for a while after the spraying and then air it out again. It kept the spiders in check for a while.

At some point we even got mosquito nets for the cots. Before that mosquitoes and spiders were a real threat to a good night's sleep. The Daddy-long-legs spiders would walk across your face and you didn't want to smash them so you just waited until they passed. One of the last years I got a war surplus jungle hammock and would put it between two trees.

We had our own generator that supplied lights to the kitchen fly (tent) and to several tents of the highest-ranking scouts. When we were at camp, this was often a sore point with other troops because we didn't always turn it off when they blew taps.

We had a Scoutmaster but the older kids, like Ward Cowan, (I think he was called Junior Assistant Scoutmaster) ran the troop most of the time. One year our Scoutmaster couldn't come to our one-week camp so we went without one. The leaders of the camp found out we had no adult with us and offered the services of the Water Front Director, for a fee. We said, "No thanks, we can't afford it." They offered him for nothing and we declined again. They told us that the first time we got in trouble we were out of there. We took that as a challenge and did everything better than the other troops that were there with their Scoutmasters.

The first year we went to Camp Norseland, we found a lot of arrowheads on the beach. So many in fact, that we started to turn them in for a display. We also found many imperfect ones and decided that this was where they were made. The imperfect ones were simply discarded. Someone found a stone with a hole in it that could have been used to drip water onto hot flint. This was one method of making the arrowheads.

Phil Cowan and I did a lot of things together. At one of our camps, we were going across the lake in canoes to spend the night on the other shore with a minimum of provisions. I don't remember what award we were trying to get but we were told how to use the two canoes as a shelter by propping them up using the paddle in a crisscross fashion. We had some sort of a tarp to put across the canoes in case it rained. In the middle of the night I turned over and dislodged a paddle so the two canoes came crashing down. One of the gunnels came down across Phil's neck.

I don't know how fast I progressed through the ranks but when I look back at the requirements, it must have taken the better part of a year for each of the advances. Even getting the Tenderfoot rank involved learning the scout oath and law, care of the flag and knot tying. The Second Class required First Aid knowledge, beginning Morse code, building a fire, and knowledge of the compass. We also had to cook a quarter pound of meat and two potatoes on an open fire without cooking utensils.

Lin Barnes was our Patrol Leader so he took me on a hike to pass some of the requirements. I built a fire (only two matches were allowed) and would have had no difficulty had someone told me not to bring hamburger. As it was I had a terrible time keeping it on a stick and out of the ashes. Lin was a good guy and ate the mess so I could pass.

The First Class rank involved some advanced First Aid, swimming 50 yards, sending 16 letters per minute of Morse code, and a 14-mile hike with a report of observations.

Once I passed the First Class rank I could begin to get merit badges toward the Star, Life, and Eagle ranks. Twenty one were needed for Eagle with 12 mandatory badges that included Life Saving, path finding, and civics. Many of these were obtainable only at camp. One year a group of us took path finding together from a Scout from Australia. We spent an hour a day for a week with him and at the end of the week, he flunked all of us and said we were a sorry bunch of scouts.

I received my Eagle award with Lin Barnes, Phil Cowan, Wendell Johnson, John Kolling, and Ken Uhlhorn. The awards were presented to us by Governor Luther Youngdahl on Sunday June 12, 1950, at the dedication of

Camp Norseland. I later received an Eagle Palm and The Order of the Arrow.

During my last year in the Scouts, we formed a Senior Explorer Troop, which was open to 15 year olds and up. We set up shop in the basement of the band shell and moved the necessary paraphernalia from the municipal building. We were told this was a mistake because the old troop needed our leadership. They were probably right because I can't remember doing anything spectacular as an Explorer. I don't know how it would have turned out because the flood destroyed everything in the band shell.

The Scouts not only provided a lot of learning and fun but the also satisfied my military desires. By the time I got old enough for the military I didn't need to go because I had already done that. Later on, I decided I didn't need men's clubs for the same reason.

The Flood

No one expected the flood in 1951. Other years the low land near the river would flood but never a town along the river. That year we had so much snow there was no place to put it. When the snow melted it melted too fast and the Blue Earth River and the Minnesota River crested at the same time in Mankato. When it started to look bad, the call went out for volunteers to build a dike on McKinley Avenue, at the north end of town. I took a shovel and went there for however long it was that we worked on the dike. The Red Cross and the Salvation Army were there. The Red Cross was selling cigarettes, gloves, and snacks. The Salvation Army was giving away the same things. The Municipal building was set up for free meals so I went there to eat. I was standing in line waiting for a meal when someone asked me to put a Red Cross armband on my arm. I did and watched as someone with a moving picture camera took our picture. I didn't realize it at the time but we were shown on TV as Red Cross workers who had come to help. I was back at work when someone noticed water coming down the street from the south. The river had already come through town and no one was at the south end of town. We all left to go home to help rescue things in our house. I helped Dad carry things from the main floor to the second floor. As it turned out that was a mistake because our first floor remained dry. We should have been taking things out of the basement because all that was lost. Dad took mother, Ann, and Corky to Minneapolis in the Buick to stay with Irv and Rufine. I was told to stay as long as I could to carry things upstairs and then drive the DeSoto over to Mankato. Bill was in the army and I considered the DeSoto to be mine. I was told to take the fan belt off so the fan wouldn't throw water on the distributor and kill the engine. It was a good thing I did because it turned out that we were at a high point in town and I had to drive through water that was higher than my tail pipe. I got a room at the Saulpaugh Hotel. There was much help needed on the Mankato side of the river so we worked days and nights. I helped evacuate people that lived near Sibley Park. I was riding on the back of a truck when some new helpers showed up. One was a classmate of mine, Jerry Childs. He asked who were we moving and I had to tell him that it was his folks. I went back to North Mankato a couple of times with these trucks and saw our teacher, Mr. Fitterer in hip boots pulling a small boat down the middle of Belgrade Ave.

Families were pretty disorganized and there was a long list of 'missing' people that was read on the radio. Actually no lives were lost but people lost track of each other. My name was read once but I didn't hear it. I was staying at the Saulpaugh Hotel and my dad found me there. He wanted me to move to the Ben Pay, where he was staying. I went to pay for two nights but they told me I had only been there one night. I remembered getting up twice but I had lost track of time and just got up when I was rested.

The Nation Guard was called out but it wasn't Mankato's because they had been nationized and sent to Alabama en-route to Korea with my brother included. The Guard that did come brought some amphibian vehicles called Ducks. They were used to show dignitaries around the flooded area. Since there was no emergency help to be done, it seemed like quite a waste to me. Especially when I heard that the Ducks were no match for the current and couldn't stay in the streets. They bumped into houses and knocked over a whole block of rural type mail boxes.

We were out of the house for several weeks and access to North Mankato was controlled. I went to a high school dance with Julie Williams and had to get to some clothes. I got a permit and went to the house to get one of my dad's suits because I didn't have one. The power was off and I couldn't see very well in his closet. I got one of his oldest ones. This didn't matter to me but the pants were about 4" to big around the middle. I could fold the pants over and hide it with the suit coat. Julie's mother had a gathering at her house for a few of Julie's friends and their dates before the dance. It was warm in the house and she wanted me to take my coat off. I refused but she could see that I was uncomfortable.

The cleanup after the floodwaters receded was the worst part. Our basement not only filled with water but the floor heaved and the water all came in at once along with a dump truck full of silt. I know how much silt there was because it all came from under our garage and it took that much sand to fill the hole. We didn't know about the hole until I noted that there was no dirt in the floor drain. I put a rake handle in the hole to see how deep the hole was and the handle couldn't reach the bottom. There were holes like that in a lot of places in town. One swallowed a road grader. A picture of it was in the paper with it's top even with the street.

We tried to shovel the silt out a basement window but it was too heavy. Bill Tanley came by and told my dad he would bring a lift pump for him. With the pump we could use city water to hose the silt into the pump and the slurry would be carried to the street. The city water was not for drinking because it was so heavily chlorinated that it was used to disinfect.

I remember the two of us trying to carry an old soaked mattress up the stairs. It was really heavy.

The flood marked an end to my Boy Scout activities, my job at the drug store, and my going to high school (a month early). In short, it was the end of a lot of things. The beginning of the next phase of my life would have to wait, however, until the end of that memorable summer.

The Summer after High School

Cleaning up after the flood was taking a long time so Dick Ryan and I decided to take a week off and go 'up north'. He had a beautiful Model A with a rumble seat. We took the seat out and filled it with provisions for a week along with a tent and sleeping bags. We didn't intend to buy anything except gas. I don't know how much money he took but I had very little. We first went to a little town over by Northfield where Dick knew a girl by the name of Carol Schidke. She had a friend and the four of us went for a ride in his car. We had to take our supplies out of the trunk so her friend and I sat on a cooler back there.

We left there at dusk and drove north not knowing where we were going. It was a good feeling. It was getting late when we got to the Cities so I looked at a map to see if a lake was near by. I spotted the first lake north of St. Paul and we headed for it. It was called White Bear Lake. It was known to everyone except Dick and me as a rich suburb of St. Paul. There was a lake there and a park so we decided to put the tent up in the park. There was a cop in town doing rounds of the store locks so we asked him if we could stay in the park. He said, "Is that a fella with ya?" When Dick said yes, the cop told us it was all right. Things have sure changed. We put up the tent and went looking for some wood to build a fire. The park was picked clean so we had to tear some wood off a dock to make a fire.

When we woke up in the morning, we saw a stream of new big cars going by on their way to work and the park looked like someone's front yard. We didn't stay long. We headed for Mission Lake. I told Dick I knew of a lake where we could rent a boat. I also told him that the last time I was there, I got some good bass bites at dusk using frogs. We had no trouble finding everything including some frogs. We went out in the boat with flashlights ready for some big bass. As soon as we put the frogs in the water we had bites but couldn't hook them no matter what we tried. Finally I said I'm going to let the next one swallow it. That worked but when I got it in the boat it turned out to be a bullhead. I didn't know there were bullheads in that lake; after all it was 'up north'. We kept a bunch anyway and went to find a place to put the tent up. We went down an old logger's trail to the Mississippi River just a few miles away. The woods were so thick that we put the tent up right in the middle of the trail. When I told Dick about bears in the woods, he got a big monkey wrench out of the car and kept it by him all night. All went well until morning when we were awakened by a truck that wanted to go somewhere down the trail. We got out of the tent and talked to the driver. After he found out we had fish for breakfast, he stayed to have some. I don't know what he chewed them with because he only had a few teeth in his head.

After our great fishing expedition we headed for Duluth. Dick knew a girl there and besides it was a nice place to visit. We were exploring the downtown area when we had a scare. We were coming down the steepest hill in town heading for the main street going across it (I think it was Superior) when the rear axle broke. This doesn't sound bad unless you know that the brakes alone weren't going to stop us. It was like someone stepped on the gas pedal. We were in low gear and the engine was doing most of the braking. We got to the bottom and went through a red light with cars whizzing by to the front and rear. It took three blocks to get the car stopped. At that point a guy came running up to tell us that we had gone through a red light.

We called the girl that Dick knew and somehow we got to her house with our tent and sleeping bags. I think we took a bus. We arranged for someone to get the car and fix it while we slept in the girl's back yard. Her name was Marilyn Mahler and she had lived in North Mankato until about the seventh grade. She left before I met her but Dick said she was the most popular girl in our class. Her dad took us several places including a bathing beach while we were getting the car fixed. It is a good thing we got the car fixed when we did because a couple more days and I would have been in love with her too. She was really nice.

The rest of the trip was uneventful but we enjoyed it and talked about it years later.

I was with Dick one other time when we almost got into big trouble. He had borrowed his grandmother's car that was about a 1935 Chevy. It was a nice car and he was showing me how fast it would go across the slough in Mankato. He pulled the throttle lever out all the way thinking it might give a little more speed. It didn't but when we reached the end of the slough he attempted to push the throttle in with the palm of his hand. The throttle bent over even with the dash and we couldn't get it back in. We were coming into the curve where the street narrowed and the car was going too fast for the corner. He put the clutch in but the engine roar sounded like it was going to burn up. Luckily one of us remembered to turn off the key.

Dick Randall read somewhere that some kids in California had put a spark plug in the tail pipe of their car and could shoot flames out when it was turned on. We, had to find out if it worked so we put one in the tail pipe of John Baker's '35 Ford. It wasn't hard to put in because John had a Model T spark coil and we could use Dick' dads shop to install it. We needed wires to the tail pipe from inside the car so we just cut holes where we wanted using a welding torch with a cutting tip on it. When we finished someone said, " Where is the gas tank in this car"? We looked and found we had missed cutting a hole in it by only a couple of inches. We could hardly wait to try it out. It didn't work very well until we discovered that raw gas would come out if we shut off the engine while we were moving. It also helped to pull out the choke a ways. With this combination we could shoot a flame 10 feet behind the car. We surprised many cars that were following too closely by giving them a shot. When we cruised Front street on Friday night, cars would stay a half a block back of us.

A policeman saw the flame in the distance and chased us. When he pulled us over, he said, "What kind of a hot rod you got here, John"? John said, "It's just an ordinary '35 Ford, officer". Of course it had no hood and a big 13 was painted on the door. He then asked about the blue light on the back and we all got out to help him look for it. He finally let us go and never figured out what he had seen.

That same Model T spark plug was used in a different way. If one connection was connected to a chain that touched the ground and the other to the car frame, the whole car would be at 10 or 20 thousand volts higher than the ground. When someone would come up to the car and grab the door handle, they would get a nasty shock. The fun didn't end there because if his car was touching bumpers with another car, the second car was affected the same way. We would go to the post office where people would park just long enough to mail something and pull up behind so that the bumpers would touch. We these people would return to their own cars, they would get the shock from their own car. We would then back off or turn the coil off and watch as the people would try again to get in their cars. I wonder if they ever trusted their cars again.

Saving Money

It was time to get a job and save some money for college in the fall. I had talked to St. Olaf about working my way through there but they told me it would not be possible so I was content to go locally to Mankato State. Tuition was only $28 per quarter and I could live at home, if I could stand it.

I had many tough jobs that summer and the next. They all reminded me that I would have to go to college because I wasn't physically strong enough to earn a living doing hard labor. I worked for George Domus, a contractor who built houses. I worked for Rose Bros. Construction Co. and for the Post Office at Christmas. I de-tasseled corn, and worked at two cement block factories, and I worked forking cans at Continental Can Co. I can't remember which ones I did first or last but I remember them all.

I worked for North Star Concrete for $1.00 an hour as a laborer. They worked 10 hours a day and 5 days a week. All that sounded good but it was hard work. Most of the time I pushed a cart they called a rickshaw. It had two wheels and a long handle. Opposite the handle, there was a hook. The hook was used to attach to a jacket that held a new concrete sewer tile. I would push it to the kiln where another worker would split the jacket and release the tile onto the floor. They were easily damaged until they had cured. I would then go back and get another one. This doesn't sound too bad but walking on the concrete floors all day soon made me feet hurt. When I stopped for a break or lunch, I could hardly get started again. I didn't have to worry about quitting, however, because I got fired. They paid time and a half for all hours over 40 each week but they changed the pay period and gave us 3 checks in 2 weeks without any overtime on any of them. The workers were grumbling but did nothing. I told them I was going to confront the management and tell them to pay me the overtime money. They all wanted the same thing so we went in together and I was the spokesman. I wanted to do this to get in good with the other workers because they were kind of a rough bunch. At least one that I knew could neither read nor write. His last name was Sargent and he was the father of one of the girls that was in my grade school class. They agreed to pay and said they had intended to do it all along but they didn't need me anymore that day. I was naive   enough to go back the next day but they didn't need me that day either.

No matter, I got another similar job that day at the Hiniker Block Plant that was closer to home and paid 5 cents an hour more. Here I just loaded and unloaded concrete blocks. Sometimes I loaded them onto truck but most of the time it was just stacking them up in the yard. I worked nights here so the heat wasn't that much of a problem. I probably wouldn't have minded it so much if I had been in better physical shape but as it was I would get tired half way through my shift. The last hour, we would clean the cement mixer with a hammer and a chisel. The mixer was big enough for several of us to be in there at once but at least we could sit down. When I think back on it they didn't even have a lock out device on the button that started the mixer. Above the mixer there was a hopper that held the sand. Sometimes we would be sent up there with a shovel to clean out the last of one size sand in preparation for a change to something different. We would be up there when they would release sand into the mixer and the hole at the bottom was big enough for a person to go through. There was a pipe that ran across the hopper so I would hang onto that when they released a batch of sand into the turning mixer.

I worked with a guy there that had a nasty scar on his nose so I asked him about it. He said he tried to shoot himself with a .22 rifle but the bullet bounced off of his skull. He had a family and couldn't get any other kind of work. I understood.

John Baker had a job there, too. He was a truck

driver and I was envious of that until I saw him come in late one night after working all day. His truck had broken down and he had to move the blocks from one truck to another all by himself.

I met Ken Prihoda there. He worked indoors putting new blocks onto a pallet so they could be put in the kiln to cure. He had a lifting device that was run with compressed air so he didn't have to lift them himself. I would have liked to have had that job.

This company also tried to cheat me out of overtime by offering me a check in the middle of a week but I refused it. They denied trying to cheat me but the bookkeeper later went to work for my dad. He told my dad to tell me I was right and that he had been instructed to do it.

Working at night had some advantages. I would go to the lake every day and swim. I would get up when it got too hot in my bedroom to sleep. That was usually after about 4 or 5 hours of sleep. I usually went to Masonic Beach to swim. I had been there so many times as a guest of Randall's that they thought I was a member but my dad wasn't even a Mason. I knew most of the regulars and the fellow that was in charge. His last name was Spots and I think he was a Mankato policeman. When I wasn't working that night, we would come back after dark and swim when they were closed. We didn't have suits with us at night but we didn't need them. It was a lot more fun, somehow, without them. One night some girls found our two cars and took the clothes out of one of them. We shared the clothes that were left in the other car and chased the girls. They went to Jean Taylor's house on the lake so we went right in after them. Her mother was home and put a stop to that. I think Karene Michels was also there but I can't remember the others.

At that time, John Baker was working for George Domus who built houses. George built them one at a time complete from footings to trim. George's dad worked for him and a couple of firemen also worked when they had a day off from 24hr. shifts. John asked George if he needed more help because he knew I was out of work at the time. George said, "Yes," so John gave me a call. When I called George, he asked me if I could hang ship-lathe or was it called Sheet rock. Anyway when I said, "Sure" he told me to come to work the next day. I hung up and asked my dad what that stuff was and he told me. It was like drywall but came in two-foot widths. It was much easier to handle than four-foot widths. I didn't work for him very long. That summer was hot and I had a terrible time driving a 16-penny nail into a 2 inch board without bending it. George asked me if I could drive a truck so I said, "Yes." He took me to the place where he rented the forms to pour a basement. I was to drive the truck that belonged to the company that owned the forms. I did fine until it was time to shift. I found the truck wouldn't go into any gears without grinding them. I had heard about double clutching so I tried that and it worked. George was a nice guy but the work was too hard for me. I kept looking for other things to do.

I went to the State Employment Office in Mankato and they had just gotten a call from Rose Brothers Construction. They needed a laborer. Later I found out that they needed someone because one of their laborers had just fallen off the roof of a house. The company was out of St. Paul and tore down old houses to resell the used lumber. My only tool was a 5-foot crowbar. My foreman pronounced it like a bore. It was heavy and we had to work over our heads with it sometimes. This was the dirtiest job I ever had. We were tearing down the houses to make room for the science building that was being built for Mankato State. I wish I could imitate my foreman's accent because it was precious. He would say, "Don't break da boards, boys", whenever he heard a board cracking.

He said to me once, "What's the matter, are you afraid to die?" That was when I was hesitant to shinny up a roof rafter to take the chimney down. I, of course, said, "Yes."

One day there was a parade in town and the foreman kept asking us if we were going to take time off to go see it. He explained that he would let us go but we wouldn't get paid for the time we were away. We finally figured out that he wanted to go see so the parade. We all said that we weren't interested in the parade. At the last moment, sure enough, he said he was going to go watch it for a while and we could continue without him. We said, "OK," and as soon as he was out of sight, we all sat down and did nothing until he re-appeared.

We had a big jug of water for drinking but we all drank out of the same coffee can.

John Baker was working a half a block away putting in forms for the footings for the new Science Building. I didn't know he was working there until I saw him once at the end of a working day. I said, "Hi, John," and he stared at me for a while but didn't know who I was. I was black with dirt and he was as clean as when he went to work that morning.

Dick Randall's Summer

Dick had an awful summer that year. Besides falling out of his boat, he ground looped an airplane and flipped his new Ford convertible. Two out of the three times I was there.

I was watching the day Dick Randall fell out of his speedboat when it was going full speed. It was right in front of the Masonic Beach. He was pulling two water skiers when their ropes got tangled in the back of the boat. It didn't bother the skiers but Dick left the wheel with the throttle on high and went to the back of the boat. He stood on the back deck and bent over the back of the boat to free the ropes. Just then the boat hit a wake from another boat and he was flipped right into the water. The skiers dropped their ropes so they wouldn't run over him and he grabbed one of the ropes thinking he could pull himself back into the boat. It didn't work; he couldn't even get his head above water. We could see this gigantic rooster tail coming from him. He finally let go and we watched as the boat headed for a fishing boat with a guy and his kid in it. When the guy realized he was in trouble he ran to the front of the boat and grabbed his kid. Dick's boat hit it broadside and became airborne. The fishing boat was wooden and had the side torn off. Tom Rockey was there and had his boat and motor. There was also a girl with her boat. It might have been Gretchen Hawes and Jean Taylor. Tom and I went to get the fisherman while the girls went for Dick. When we got back the girls said Dick was still out there and we better hurry. They told us his swimming suit had been torn off and he wouldn't get in the boat with them. When we got to him he looked pretty tired. No one had life jackets, of course. The boat ran ashore at the far end of the lake and tore a hole in the bottom when it hit.

We helped tow the boat back to Dick's cabin not knowing that it had a hole in the bottom. We nearly lost it when it filled with water and sank. Fortunately it was right by his dock at the time.

Dick's dad rewarded him with a new boat. It was a Century and was bigger and faster than the old one.

Dick Randall, Jon Nordgren, and I went to Duluth just for something to do one weekend. Jon was going to rent an airplane so we could see the harbor from the air. That didn't happen for some reason. I guess they didn't have the right kind of plane available. We did find some girls, however. They worked in the telephone office and showed us around town. When it came time to sleep we drove Dick's station wagon out in the country a little way and parked. We had sleeping bags and I decided to sleep on the roof. Actually I had an air mattress also and it was quite comfortable. In the middle of the night, the lights of an oncoming train awakened me. They would sweep back and forth and were so bright that I couldn't see anything. At first

I didn't know it was a train and when I realized that it was, I got scared. I thought Dick had parked on a railroad track. I knew I had time to get down and run but I didn't which way to go and I thought it would be really tragic to run into the path of the train. About that time the train whistle began to blare as it was approaching our intersection and I could tell it was moving fast. I decided to stay put. It was a long several seconds before the train went by about 10 feet from our car. Later that night, it started to rain and I had to get down and join them in the back of the car. It all seemed like part of the fun.

Dick destroyed his new 1951 Ford convertible that summer and his dad also replaced that. I guess a lot of people were drinking Hamm's beer then. One day I drove out to Dick's place at the lake and Jimmy was with me. My dad had recently bought a 1938 Ford to replace the 1938 DeSoto that Bill had taken to service with him. It was a beautiful dark green two-door with a rebuilt V-8 engine in it. I think he paid $200 for it. It was fun to be able to just go for a ride and not need to rely on Jimmy all the time. We saw Dick and we all decided to go to the Attic but Dick had to drive, also, because I didn't want to go back out to the lake to take him home. He was following me to town and Jimmy looked back and could not see his headlights. He said, "Where is Dick?" In my all knowing attitude I said, "Oh, he probably took a short cut and will be waiting for us in town." When he wasn't in town, I assumed he had changed his mind about coming. He often did things like that. We didn't find out until the next day that he had driven in the ditch and flipped end over end when he hit a side road. He ended up in the back seat, was banged up and had a sore back. He was able to get out of the car and up to the road where he eventually stopped a car and got a ride to the hospital. We went to see the car at the Ford garage. It was flattened. Dick was lucky to be alive. When we asked him why he drove in the ditch, he said that he was looking under the dash for something.

College

I was anxious to go to college the fall after high school. My only choice was Mankato State Teachers College. We called it T.C. I was tired of high school and wanted the independence that I imagined would come with college. After all if we paid for it, we should be able to demand our money's worth. It shouldn't be like high school where we didn't pay and we were stuck with a system designed to please everyone. We would be there because we wanted to be there. There would be no time wasted on those that didn't want to be there. The professors would all be smarter than the teachers that I had had and it would be so nice, I thought. I would work hard, do my homework, read the books, keep my mouth shut. What a dreamer I was. None of the above was true.

My memories of college center on the professors rather than the courses for some reason. There were good ones and bad ones, old ones and young ones. Some were unknown and others were notorious.

I met a couple of the notorious ones the first year. Cora P. Sletton was one of them. Even my mother had heard of her. She taught geography and was still thrilled by the subject and taught with great enthusiasm. She did everything she could to make the subject interesting but it was still geography. She taught a lot of local geography and we were told that she walked a lot of it because she was interested in it. She told us of a secret cave in the vicinity that a student had discovered and showed to her. When he went into the service, he told her he was going to open a tourist site there and made her promise not to disclose the location. He, of course, did not survive the war and according to her the secret would die with her.

I missed her final exam somehow. I thought it was in the afternoon when it was in the morning. She saw me looking for the class and asked where I had been. She let me take the exam even though she said she had to give up an alumni tea or something to give it to me. I think she favored boys. She even let me tease her occasionally in class. She loved topographic maps and used them to teach us about local terrain. Once when the class was stumped she said we were looking at the famous cranberry bogs in Wisconsin. After that I would suggest cranberry bogs whenever we were stumped. She patiently explained why the others areas could not be cranberry bogs several times before she realized that I was pulling her leg. The girls were terrified of her and couldn't understand how I would dare do such a thing.

J.Hervy Shutts was another notorious professor. He taught biology and I took it thinking it was a science. I loved science and thought I would like biology. Nothing was further from the truth. It was all memorization of names that had origins in some other language. J. Hervy was a big, big man and had played football some place, I was told. He also had started his teaching career in a high school and brought all his high school routines with him. The first day we were to use a microscope, he had us line up and file though the adjacent room to pick up a microscope. We were told to pick it up with one hand and put the other hand under so we wouldn't drop it. I knew at that moment that we weren't going to get along. One of us was in the wrong place. I should have dropped the class instead of trying to help him.

We were dissecting a grasshopper once and I finished early. I had noticed all the important things rather quickly. I didn't even need the scalpel we were given because I cracked it open with my fingernails. Dr. Shutts was critical of my meager observations but I told him there wasn't much to a grasshopper. Someone later told me that Shutts had done his Ph.D. on the anatomy of a grasshopper.

He gave us a workbook that was like a coloring book before the colors. He told us that we were to draw all the things that we saw in the microscope in the book. He said this was our workbook and our means of study. At the end of the quarter, he asked us to turn in the workbooks for a grade. I, of course, had drawn nothing in the book. I wrote on the cover of the book that it was mine and my means of study and none of his business let alone a part of my grade. I wasn't worried because he told us that it would only make up a small percent of our grade. When he gave it back, he had given me a red minus f with a circle around it. That was the equivalent of a minus 4. If I hadn't turned it in, it would have been a 0 and taken my grade down only one step but a minus 4 took it from an A or B down to a D. He explained the arithmetic to me. I told him he would be happier if he went back to teaching in high school.

Even before school started that first fall I got into trouble. There was a freshman-get-acquainted get together at a local roller skating rink. I had never skated there but went with Dick Randall to see if anything of interest was happening. That means looking at the new girls. We no sooner got in when a tall, pretty girl said, "Get some skates on and have some fun. I've always been impressed by girls who are forward so at the end of the evening I asked her if she wanted a ride home. She said she had come on the bus and should go back on it. I figured another time might be better so said just said, "O.K. I'll see you later." I didn't realize at the time that it would be the next day in Algebra class. First I was happy to see her come into the room but got a real jolt when she turned out to be the teacher. I wondered if she recognized me but she gave no indication of it. Her name was Hildegarde Horeni and she turned out to be a fine teacher. The first thing she told us was that there had been a change in books. This was not welcome to me because I already had one of the old ones. It was a little white book written by Love. I think it had been my brothers. It turned out that Miss Horeni (we didn't call her anything else) used the little white book for examples of problems. This came in handy for me because the answers were all in the back of the book. One day she asked us to work on problems in class and used the little white book. I looked up the answers and spent the rest of the time looking out the window. She called on me like I expected and when I gave her the correct answers she thought I was some sort of whiz kid. She was very nice to me and even checked out some books from the library that she thought I should read. I didn't read them, of course. She broke her leg skiing that year and had to be carried to the second floor until they changed her room. I saw a music teacher (Bruce Howden) doing the honors once and found out later she married him and the two of them went on to distinguishing careers at other colleges.

I finished college algebra and ran into a strange situation the second quarter when I took trigonometry. First of all, it was the same course and book that I had had in high school. Secondly, it was taught by Chuck Blackstead. He had only recently graduated from Mankato State with a major in math. The school felt they needed him, however, because he was a magician. That doesn't seem to make sense except that the college went to high schools throughout Minnesota to "recruit" high school students. There were only about 1300 students enrolled at T.C. and there was a feeling that more were needed to establish Mankato as the logical alternative to the University of Minnesota. These recruiting trips involved a troupe of college students with special skills that would impress the high school students. Chuck Blackstead had been a big success as a magician so he was offered a staff position in the math department. This way he could continue with the troupe.

I took the class thinking it would be an easy class and an A for a grade. I set out to impress Chuck by helping him when he had difficulty with several problems he was working on the board. I had seen them before but he didn't know it. A few times he asked me to show the class how some problems were worked. After that he would ask me to teach the class because he was going on one of his trips to a high school. He didn't give me any time to prepare so I would ask others, like John Kolling, to take portions of the day's assignment. I would usually start while they were preparing their parts. Nobody thought it was that unusual at the time but now I look back on it as a strange way to run a college but good experience for me.

Physics

Dr. G.W. Wissink was the head of the physics department and since I majored in physics, I saw a lot of him. I enjoyed physics courses more than any other subject because it is the search for the truth about the universe. Where did it come from? What makes it work? What is going to happen to it?

Wissink taught a brand of physics that should have been called mechanics. It was taught with little or no calculus. His courses contained none of the interesting things like Cosmology, Quantum Mechanics, or Relativity. This was in spite of the fact that Quantum Mechanics and Relativity were already 20 and 45 years old respectively.

He was probably in his 40's and had been head of the science department before he took a sabbatical to work for a defense contractor during the war. He had buckteeth (much like mine) and a quick smile. He was a nice guy and has a building named for him on the new campus.

We started with a running battle, however, about homework. He assigned questions at the end of each chapter and we were to do them outside of class. When we came in with them, he would ask if we had any trouble with them. Someone would say they couldn't get number 5 and so he would do it on the board. Then someone else would say they couldn't get some other number and he would do that on the board while the class was copying them down as if they had done them at home. He would go on for most of the hour that way until all the tough ones were done and copied. Then everyone , except me, would turn them in as homework. With me it was a matter of principle (something that wouldn't have given me the same compunction in a history class). I wanted to know how to work the problems but didn't care about showing my work to Wissink. He looked at it a different way. He thought this ought to be a part of the grade. I thought the tests were given to determine grade. It reminded me of Mr. Roberts in high school history.

We also had a 2-hour lab each week that was very well prepared. I especially liked the electronics experiments that consisted of vacuum tubes, big capacitors, and transformers. We would arrange them on a 'bread-board' and make radios, amplifiers, battery chargers, speed controllers, and the like. This form of electronics was much like plumbing and one could figure out how it was to be done. I was intrigued by his dc power supply that came from a bank of Edison batteries that never wore out. Why didn't we have them in our cars, I thought. I still don't know the answer to that.

One time we were to shoot a .22 caliber bullet into a block of wood. The wood was suspended on a string and we were to calculate the speed of the bullet from the height reached by the block of wood as it swung from the impact. Unfortunately this block of wood had been used too many times and the bullet went through the wood to the black board where it shattered the slate.

These classes were interesting for me but he insisted on a write-up of the experiment according to a format he had prepared. This was a good idea and I did a few but that part wasn't very much fun and I wasn't learning anything from it so I soon stopped doing them. Wissink soon noticed the missing homework and write-ups from the lab. He confronted me several times but by then I had shown that I could get all A's in the tests so I wanted to prove a point. He gave me an A that quarter but said he would lower my grade one letter without them the next quarter. I said B's are fine with me. He gave me a B that next quarter but when I continued my pattern into the third quarter, he said he would give me a C if I didn't do the homework. I didn't and he did. The first year I had a B average and thought I had won. The next year, he got even meaner and gave me a D in the fall. Worse yet, with only a week left in the second quarter, he said he would give a failing grade even though I continued to get A's and B's in all his tests. He had won. I went home and did all the homework for the quarter in a weekend. When I handed it in he accused me of having it all done as we went but refusing to turn them in. We had quite a talk and at some point I said I could send my little sister up to copy the problems off the board after he had done them if that was what he wanted. He gave me an A that quarter.

We were taking a test one day and I looked across the street to the Court House and saw them towing cars away that were illegally parked there. Mine was going to be towed soon so I asked Wissink if I could go rescue it. After a moment of hesitation he let me go. When I got back, I could see he was still in a bad mood so I asked about it. He accused me of watching them tow his car away without saying anything and then running over to save mine. I hadn't, of course, and he knew it. He was still bitter, however.

I took the rest of his courses without a problem and he turned out to be my best ally when it came to going to graduate school. He wrote letters about me that sounded like he was talking about someone else.

Wissink wasn't the only one in the physics department, When I was a junior I took thermodynamics from a new member of the staff named David Bushnell. He was the opposite of Wissink. He talked only in math terms. He would go to the board and say, "ds by dy over dp by dt gives dx or something like that. He never told us what the letters stood for or why he was setting up an equation that way. I learned to copy and repeat but learned nothing. I wish there had been a compromise between Wissink's 'no-math' and Bushnell's 'no- explanation'.

Outside of School

My life was divided between college, work, dating, and living at home. It was hard to know where to put the emphasis when there wasn't enough time to do justice to all. I didn't try very hard to please my folks during this time so it wasn't much fun living at home. Work was essential because nothing else was possible without it. The biggest problem with it was that it took up valuable time. College was needed to get a good job and dating was fun so it got top priority.

The first year of college I worked as a janitor in a small office building in North Mankato. I think it was a converted church. That went fine until the owner asked me to work Saturdays at his store in Mankato. I forget what he sold because all he wanted me to do was clean the basement. It hadn't been touched in at least 20 years and I got most of it cleaned before I got angry. He didn't mention this kind of work when he hired me and it was filthy work. I finally complained to him and got no sympathy so I told him to find someone else to do it. I think there were times after that that I had no job and found having no money wasn't much different than having very little money. Sometimes Dad even let me charge some gas to him.

I met Joanne Larson (Jo) at a sock hop at the beginning of my second year. It was the first year for her even though she had come in the summer and taken some courses then. I still couldn't dance but managed to hide it for a couple of dances before I asked if she would like to go out to Paul's. I was with Dick Randall and she was with Hisako Nagata. Hisako (Sox) knew Dick because he drove his new convertible for a parade when Sox was the homecoming queen. Sox was trying to introduce Jo to Dick but I kept getting in the way. We went to Paul's and I liked her right away so I decided to go steady with her if she would let me. It didn't happen right away but we didn't go with anyone else seriously after that.

I spent all my spare time with Jo. She lived first at Kent House. There were about 20 girls that lived there with the Kents in an old building near the campus. It had been a hospital at one time. The Kents had strict rules but little ability to enforce them. I would come in the front door and hide a cigarette in the palm of my hand because smoking was not allowed. Mrs. Kent could smell it and come to the top of the second floor stairs, where they lived, and ask if I was smoking. I would say, "no." There were lots of nice girls there and they had a good time with there own parties. Jo's first roommate was Hisako Nagata (Sox). She was from Hawaii and was the homecoming queen the fall I met Jo. Later Jo moved to an apartment upstairs in a house in North Mankato with three other girls so they could cook their own meals. The Griebels owned the house and were nice to the girls. They owned a small grocery store a block away on Belgrade.

Sometimes Jo and I would wash dishes for my mother and she would give us 50 cents. That was enough for two beers at Paul's Place. We spent a lot of time there and could nurse a beer for most of the evening. Marge and Hank were the owners and ran the place by themselves. It was a popular place for college kids even though none were over 21 (the legal limit then). It was out of town on the way to St. Peter and the sheriff didn't come because there was never any trouble there. Marge and Hank saw to that. Marge was tiny and walked very fast. She would often carry 10 or 12 empty beer bottles at a time. Hank was quiet but his presence helped keep order. Jo and I spent a lot of time there and even did some math homework under the weak green lights that lit the booths.

I saw Dave (Jimmy) Nielsen there one night and watched him put four balls in a row on a pin ball machine that paid him $5. Dave spent some time in Mankato even though he still went to St. Olaf. The machine took nickels and pay-outs were illegal but happened under the counter.

This sticks in my memory because I was addicted to this machine and had been trying for months to get a winner.

I lost my wallet once and didn't miss it. Someone found it in the street in front of Kent House (where Jo lived) and turned it in at the school. The school notified me to pick it up at the office. When I went to pick it up the clerk said the good news is that the wallet was found but the bad news was that the money was gone. I said, "What money? There was no money in it."

Once, when I ran out of money, I set pins after not doing it for many years. I set two alleys for two shifts and it nearly killed me. I could barely walk afterwards. I was so slow I couldn't stop to get a drink of water even between shifts. That was the last time I set pins.

I got a job as a janitor in the new science building the second year of college. It paid 60 cents an hour and was limited to 20 hours a week. I liked this job and it provided beer money but I still had to work between quarters stacking concrete blocks or what ever else I could find to pay for tuition. Tuition was 28 dollars including the $8 activity ticket. I decided I could get along without the activity ticket that was mostly admission to the football and basketball games. I talked to a lot of people who couldn't let me register for 20 dollars. I was finally sent to the dean of instruction (A.B. Morris). He told me the library was also included in the activity ticket so I agreed not to go there. At that point he told me that even though it was a separate tuition, it wasn't separable from the academic part.

When I wasn't working, or dating Jo, or eating and sleeping at home, I was in school. Not always in class, however. Sometimes I was in the Union. It was nice to see a lot of my high school friends come in there. Some were from classes that had graduated a year or two before me while others were from my class. A few had been with me all the way back to grade school and many were from North Mankato. Karen Oversea was Queen of some event (I forget which one). Jon Nordgren was there, as was Al LaFrance.

We played a lot of cards in the Union. That was where we found out about things that were going on. We played Hearts or Buck Euchre and always for money. It was no secret because there was money on the table. At some point the Governor closed the Union because of the gambling, which was illegal throughout the state. We thought some kid lost some of his spending money there and told his folks who complained to the Governor. Anyway we had to go to the squash courts to play for a while. I remember John Just caught someone dealing off the bottom of the deck. John threw his hand back to him and told him to deal off the top. I didn't know who this guy was because he had just transferred from the University of Minnesota. The guy re-dealt without complaining. I was impressed. Of course we all dealt off the bottom if a quick peek at the bottom card didn't please us.

Chemistry

Chemistry was pretty interesting to me and I ended up majoring in it as well. I finished this major thinking that I could always get a job as a bench chemist but didn't know of many places that hired a physics major. I was wrong about that but didn't know it at the time. There were only two chemistry professors, Dr. Leonard Ford and Dr. Alvin Walz. Ford was head of the science and Math Division and everyone called him Father Ford, except to his face. Walz was young and this may have been his first teaching job. He was in charge of most labs. I spent a lot of time in labs because I liked them. I was fascinated at the way things reacted to make other things in a predictable way.

My freshman year I had trouble getting to 8 o'clock classes on time. I usually arrived at about 8:10 and came in late. Ford was teaching freshman chemistry at 8 o'clock and lectured me about coming late. One day he said he was going to lock the door at 8:05 the next day. When I came late the next day, sure enough, the door was locked. I knocked on the door until he opened it. He said nothing. A couple of years later when he was teaching physical chemistry, he was having a bad day and was making a lot of small mistakes on the board. I was calling his attention to them as they happened and it was getting embarrassing. The rest of the class was getting nervous when Ford turned around and said, "I tend to give A's to those who find mistakes on the board." It was a pleasant surprise to me and quite a shock to those that were afraid to speak up when they saw the mistakes. Ford was not a good teacher. He did little or no preparation because he had taught the same thing so many times. He seemed distant like he was interested in things more important.

Walz was more fun. I could tease him and get him to smile. Once I broke a glass tube trying to get a rubber stopper twisted onto the end of it. The broken tube went into the palm of my hand and cut a small vein. The blood went up the tube (about 2 inches) and slowly ran out the top. It didn't hurt so I showed it to several students who nearly fainted. I then went looking for Walz. He told me to take it to a Doctor. He knew there was a Doctor who was giving shots to kids at the Lab (elementary) school across the street. When I got to the doctor, he looked at my hand for about 2 seconds and said why doesn't someone pull that tube out of there? He then proceeded to do it. That was the end of my fun.

I didn't like organic chemistry because it involved too much memorization. I hated memorization. Walz taught organic chemistry and I had trouble staying awake in his class. He complained at me several times before I told him he was just putting the stuff on the board that appeared in the book. I suggested that if he told me when the tests were given and the pages that it covered in the book, I wouldn't need to come to class. He gladly took me up on the idea. I wish I could report that I did well but I didn't. I kept putting off the memorization until the day before the test and there was too much to learn in one day. I repeated one of these quarters to bring up my grade but didn't do much better the second time. I decided I wouldn't become an organic chemist.

Summers were welcome. I didn't take courses and my janitor job was suspended until fall. That meant looking for the best paying summer jobs I could find. I've already mentioned tearing old houses down and constructing new ones. I also mentioned the concrete plant jobs but I also worked on the assembly line at Minnesota Automotive, I worked at Continental Can and I spent a summer cutting grass at a gasoline tank farm.

The assembly line at Minnesota Automotive was nice. I got to sit down at some of the workstations and we rotated every hour. I thought it was such a nice place, I got my brother a job there. Actually I just told him about an opening for a draftsman and he did the rest. We sometimes carpooled because we were both living at home. The problem was that Bill was usually late for work and we were suppose to punch a clock. I did it faithfully but Bill stopped using it altogether. When it came time to prepare a two-week paycheck, the paymaster came to Bill and told him there would be no pay for him. Bill went to the manager and said, "Here is my work. Keep me or let me go but I don't punch time clocks. The manager kept him but it was his mistake because Bill had his job in a couple of years.

I worked at Continental Can Company one of those summers but probably not for a whole summer. I had more jobs than there were summers. Everybody wanted to work at CCC because they paid pretty well. It was between $1.50 and $2.00 per hour. Many teachers in town worked there for the summer and had many of the good jobs because the came back every year.

I started out stacking bags of cans into boxcars on the railroad tracks. The first day we were told to walk down the tracks until we found a foreman and check in with him. After that we belonged to that foreman and he put us on his list. We reported to him each day after that. I knew a kid that was wise to this procedure so he never did report to a foreman. Instead he just kept walking down the tracks until he couldn't be seen. He simply went back home or to the golf course from there. At night he would come back up the tracks to our dressing room where he would punch the clock just like the rest of us. I think he did this all summer.

As soon as he could, my foreman introduced me to forking cans. They called it forking because we used a tool that looked like an old-fashioned grass rake with wooden tines on it that were pointed like a fork. With that we could pick up 8 or more cans at a time (depending on how wide the fork was). At first I was 'bulk forking' cans which meant I put them directly into a railroad car. The pace was a little slower than inside so it was a good place to learn. When I graduated to 'indoor forking' I put them into bags about 3' x 3' x 3'. I even worked putting the bags in place for a while. The pace at either of these jobs was set to go as fast as one could possible go. The noise from the cans was so loud that we couldn't talk to each other. The foreman would gesture instead. Time would pass very slowly. We had a break at mid-morning and at mid-afternoon. If we wanted more than that we could fake needing a rest room break. They were wise to this so they had removed the doors to the toilet stalls and one had to go there and sit down in order to get a smoke break. One day a toilet was overflowing and water was running out onto the work floor. A foreman ran into the men's room to check this out and found Neal Donaldson sitting on a toilet next to the one that was overflowing. He was just sitting there smoking a cigarette. When the foreman asked him what was going on, he said, "How should I know, I ain't no plumber." His attitude was perfect for the job. Mine wasn't and I could hardly wait until it was time to go back to school.

I was back working in a boxcar when I developed an infection in a cut near my wrist. When the vein turned blue, I knew it was blood poisoning. I didn't know how serious it could be but I went to the company nurse who sent me to a doctor in town. There I got a Penicillin shot and some pills and was told to go back to the nurse to get hot compresses. It was labor-day weekend and I sat in the nurse's office Saturday, Sunday, and Monday getting time and a half for Saturday and double time for Monday and Tuesday. I thought I had gone to heaven. When they decided that I could go back to work they sent me out along the boxcars to pick up cans that had fallen on the ground. That only lasted for a couple of days and when they said I could go back to my regular job, I quit.

Starting school each fall was a hassle because it wasn't only a matter of picking the classes that I wanted but many were full by the time I signed up. I was assigned an advisor but never used him. I simply picked the classes I wanted and signed his name. Thank goodness I knew Mary Meyer because she worked in the Registrar's office and helped me get into the classes that I needed. By the time classes started, many students would have made changes so spaces would open. She would find one of these openings for me. She even made out a duplicate IBM card one time to get me in.

Required Courses

I didn't care which of the required courses I took each quarter because I had to take them sometime anyway. Required courses were all a waste of time and my attitude toward them was so bad that I seldom read the assignments and usually got bad grades. The idea was good, however. T.C. was a college that was primarily dedicated to producing teachers and it was felt that teachers should have a well-rounded education. Like most good ideas, however, it didn't work in actual practice. Taking courses in fields that are of little interest usually produces antagonism toward that field. Partly because of the time required that had to be taken away from the courses of primary interest. Any knowledge gained was quickly forgotten because it was learned only to pass a test at the end of the course.

One of the first courses I took the first year was Health. My teacher was Miss Weblemoe and she was called sexy Web. Mostly because she was anything but sexy. One of the first days she was teaching us how a classroom of students could all wash their hands with one bar of soap and a pitcher of water. I started to walk out when she asked where was I going. I told her I must have gotten in the wrong class by mistake. I told her I was looking for Health 101 and she said, "This is Health 101." I sat down again but couldn't believe it. A few days later, we had a new instructor, I can't remember his name and no one told us why the switch had been made.

I finally found a used book that I bought from Jeanne Audrey Powers for 50 cents. She had bought it new for over $5.00. I used to marvel at the people that bought new books. Of course the returning vets got them with their G.I. Bill. I read parts of the book and earned about a B in the class. It was really a terrible course but I was still being somewhat tolerant with school in general. That was until I got my grade and it said I got a D. I went to the instructor to point out his error and he told me that I had missed 10 classes and that he took a 1/3 of a grade off for each one over the 4 that he allowed. It was, he said just like he had told us the first day. Of course he didn't tell us that because we had a different instructor the first day. I came close to getting into real trouble that day. His office was in the Physical Education Building and he had a basketball sitting on his desk. I had my hands on it when he told my about the grade calculation. I could picture how that ball would look smashed against his face. Somehow I resisted. There was another student there that had the same problem but his grade had gone down to an F. We went to the Dean of instruction to complain. The other student had been gone because his mother had died and this failing grade prevented him from graduating because it was a required course. I went with him but kept my mouth shut because his problem was much worse than mine. A.B. Morris listened to our case and then concluded that it was just tough. We could repeat the course and bring our grade up. My overall attitude toward T.C. began to deteriorate that day. It wasn't helped by any of the other required courses.

Physical education was on the list of required courses. I forgot how many hours we had to have but it seemed silly to me that teachers had to be able to run and jump. I don't think Art was required so evidently they didn't have to know how to draw or paint. I've often wondered how physical games became such a big part of an education. To me, they are wonderful as separate things and should have nothing to do with getting an education. I took tennis, archery, track (which I had to drop), handball, and apparatus. Apparatus includes the high bar, the parallel bars, the horse, the rings, and other tools of gymnastics. I took it from C.P. Blakeslee. I don't know what his first name was but he was an institution at T.C. I think he used to be head coach of the major sports. Some athletic field is now named for him. He was patient with me and got a bang out of me trying to do things on the high bar. He didn't appreciate it, however, when I told him I was too busy to help him with some upcoming meet. He expected me to time and measure other athletes' accomplishments. That would have represented the epitome of everything I detested. He lectured me on the need to give to others. It lowered my opinion of him.

I got a good grade in archery because we got to keep our own scores. Handball was fun and strenuous. I used to come out of the courts beet red. I took tennis from 'Rummy' Macias. He was the wrestling coach and didn't make us work too hard at tennis. I think we just hit balls back and forth in the gym. I signed up for track and softball (6 weeks of each) but had to drop the course because Bob Otto, the teacher and head football coach, had us run the 60 yard dash one of the first days without any warm up. I hadn't run anywhere for years. I stretched my quadriceps so badly in the 60 yard run, I could hardly walk. We weren't going to get along anyway because he started each class with calisthenics in the indoor track. When he asked us to get down on our backs on the recently watered cinder track, I just stood there and glared at him. I had clean gym clothes on and knew better. When I dropped his class I told him several things he didn't want to hear. I'm glad I didn't have to play football for him.

I don't remember why I took speech. I don't think it was required but maybe it was on the list of courses that were accepted for substitution for English courses. I took the course from Vernon Beckman. He wasn't a Ph.D. so we didn't called him Doctor Beckman and I know we didn't call him Vernon so I don't know what we called him. I don't remember him ever telling us how to make speeches, he just listened to them and then criticized the things that were wrong. That method of teaching seemed to be the rule rather than the exception at T.C. I liked speech and did well except for one speech. The speeches were divided into different topics and humor was the one I thought I could do better than anyone else. I prepared a long list of canned jokes that I had used successfully before. I started with a big smile and bigger expectations. When joke after joke fell flat, I got more and more disturbed and finally angry. I finally sat down without finishing. Beckman asked if I wanted to finish at another time and I said. "Not for this group." I knew then that being a comedian was not in my future. Maybe a politician would be just as bad, I thought.

It was a bad experience that taught me a lot. I was getting an education in a lot of things that I hadn't expected but little in the things I did expect.

I did take a couple of English courses but none were on grammar. I think as a freshman we could test out of some of the required English courses. I took one English course from Robert Wright. It was on composition and we had to turn in an umpteen-word paper on a subject of our choosing.

I used one I had written in high school. It was on perfume and got and A in high school chemistry. Wright wasn't quite so impressed and gave me a B. I used it in another class (I forget which one) and got a C. All three instructors found different things wrong with it.

The other English course I took was at night and was taught by Effie Hunt and she was a sweetheart. It was the first course I took at night and found it was full of teachers that were getting extra credits toward a degree they didn't have. The first night Dr. Hunt asked all of us to tell the class about the things that we read routinely. She started in the front row and each one told a bigger lie by starting with all the things that had already been mentioned and adding one of their own. Everyone read the New York papers and literary magazines.

I was sitting in the back row wondering what I was going to do. When she finally got to me I said I read the comics everyday in the newspaper. She said that she did too and asked about my favorites. We shared several favorites before everyone else added the comics to their lists but it was too late for them. We had pulled one off on the others and we got along famously after that. I heard she later became a Dean at Indiana State University.

I hated history more than any other of the required courses and had to repeat the course called 'Ancient and Medieval History'. I had the same instructor the second time and when he called me in to find out why I was doing poorly the second time, he discovered that I didn't have a book. He lent me one of his that was an older edition. We had daily quizzes and exchanged papers with a neighbor for correcting. I had a friend who used to fill in blanks for me but the answers were read too fast. We couldn't fill in enough answers to get a good grade. After the final, I went to see him because he had made a mistake correcting my paper. When I first walked in, he congratulated me for getting a B. I pointed out, however, that he counted the red checks wrong and I actually did worse than he had determined. He agreed and gave me a D. He said he didn't understand why I had come in. I had strange principles.

I like history now but only on topics that interest me. I would have liked to read a little about Mankato history in college but I wasn't interested in the Huns sweeping across Europe. I didn't even know what a Hun was.

I had to take a course called Industrial Arts Education but the name meant nothing. It was a common sense course on how many mechanical things worked. One day the instructor, Richard Kohler, was telling us how an automatic transmission worked. At some point he said, "--- and then the oil solidifies and blah, blah, blah." I almost choked. I couldn't help myself and told him and everyone else that oil doesn't solidify under any circumstances.

Elective Courses

In addition to the required courses, we chose other courses outside of our majors and minors. They were called electives. I enjoyed one of these called 'engineering drawing' even though I wasn't a natural at it. I took it from Ira Johnson and he was good. I was proud of the finished product and got better with each 'plate' (that's what a drawing was called). No matter how good my plates were, Ira would find something wrong. We even had to ink some of them and a smudge would ruin the whole thing. During the third quarter we learned descriptive geometry where a plate could be drawn with projections on them that could depict another dimension like folding the paper. This was handy for drawing things like water pipes that ran in straight lines but got deeper in the ground with increasing length. The drawing could be used to determine the length of the pipe needed. By coincidence, I was taking a math course called Solid Analytical Geometry that did the same thing without the drawing. Ira would give us a grade based on how close we had come to the length of the pipe that he determined from his drawing. On one occasion I said I deserved a better grade because I was closer than he was. He wanted to know how I knew that so I showed him how to calculate the exact distance and he seemed disappointed that his method had been bettered.

Phil Cowan was in my class and sat in front of me, just like in 6th grade. He had spent the previous summer in a one-man fire tower in Montana. He had reserved a two-man tower for the next year and asked me if I wanted to go there with him. I told him I would but he got drafted before we had the chance.

I think it was in the second year of college that I was involved in an automobile accident that ruined my pretty green Ford. I was coming across the bridge to North Mankato when the cars in front of me stopped. I had my foot on the brake but it didn't do much good because of the mechanical brakes that it had. I hit the back of a '49 Ford station wagon with it's brakes on and two people in the front. I mention all that because the rear bumper of that car was so far off the road that my bumper and bumper guards never touched it. Instead, my grill hit it and smashed it into my radiator. A second later a car hit the back of my car and damaged my trunk and right fender. I continued to drive the car for some time after that but the grill was gone, the front fenders were smashed and the radiator had to be pinched shut with pliers in places. The right rear fender was so bad that it had to be taken off. The insurance company covering the car behind me eventually paid for my car but it was hard finding another car that I liked as much as that one.

I found out that it was going to cost too much to get it fixed so I began looking for a replacement as soon as I got the insurance settlement. I found a '40 Plymouth 4-door that seemed functional but wasn't in perfect condition. The paint wasn't shiny like the Ford. Perhaps it had been repainted. I bought it anyway and liked the hydraulic brakes. The car actually stopped when they where applied.

The engine was only a straight six instead of a V8 which was not as satisfying but was sufficient. It had a three speed manual transmission (three on the tree, as they called it}. Jo learned to drive it with ease but hadn't wanted to start with the Ford. Perhaps she felt I was too protective of the Ford. I did polish it all the time. Even the dash had many coats of wax and looked like real wood even though it was metal.

I wasn't content to sell the Ford to a junk dealer because I would not have gotten much for it. I sold it in parts instead. This did not make Dad very happy because it sat beside the house in various states of disassembly. I got quite a bit of money for the engine. I sold it to one of the Kelly brothers who put it in a home built speedboat. He also bought the dash but I did not ever see it in place.

After the second quarter of my sophomore year (I had the required 90 quarter hour credits), Jon Nordgren and I went to Minneapolis to take the tests for getting into the Naval Air Corps. John had taken me flying many times and I had handled a plane enough to know that I liked it. Jon's brother-in-law was the airport manager and his Dad had friends who owned airplanes. We got to fly them just for paying for the gas and oil. Some of them burned considerable amounts of oil. One was a P.T. 19. It was a military trainer used during the war. It was an all-aluminum, low-wing airplane and had a sliding cockpit canopy. I was with Jon once in that plane when the engine quit. It started again when Jon switched to the other ignition system. There were gauges in the back seat, where I sat, but the plane vibrated so badly that I couldn't read any of them. Jon was a good pilot by then and I had second thoughts about joining up with others that could already fly but I went anyway. I hadn't signed any commitment when we went for the tests.

We took written tests all day and we both passed easily. My eyes were tested even before the written tests and were found to be perfect. I thought the rest of the physical exam would be a snap but I failed the dental exam (of all things). He told me I had nose and pallet structure that was too narrow. He said I would have trouble breathing oxygen through my nose. He was right. My smoking habit had caused my nasal passages to swell almost shut. Anyway I flunked. Jon went on without me and crashed two years later. I went back to school with mixed feelings and decided to stay out of the military as long as I could. I had already taken the college deferment tests and decided to keep up my grades to evade or at least postpone the draft. I felt I had given 'them' their chance and now 'they' would have to come for me with a net.

I think it was the third year of school when my brother came back from the University of Minnesota and took some classes at T.C. When he got out of the army he went to the University of Minnesota but soon ran out of money. We took physics together at T.C. and decided to share a book. When mid-quarter exams were approaching, I asked Bill for the book so I could study for the exam. He said, "I thought you had the book."

Between my junior and senior years in college, I got a job at Great Lakes Pipe Line. It was a large tank farm south of town that stored and distributed gasoline and other petroleum products that came from a refinery by way of a pipeline. My job was mostly to cut grass but they had an excess of employees with little to do. They were there in case there was a fire. They didn't tell us that but with the training we got in fire fighting we figured it out. I worked with John Baker who had worked there the year before and taught me all the ropes. I would have worked there the year before but the employees had to be 21 years old. I told John about the job the year before because he was a year older than I was.

Jo's brother drove a gasoline truck and would fill up there. This was tame for him because he had driven an ammunition truck in Germany during the war. I talked to him occasionally when the boss wasn't looking.

There was only one boss and he ran the office help as well as the grounds keepers. Everyone kept track of his whereabouts. He drove around in a green Chevy panel truck so we would watch for it. He usually went to a nearby eatery for a break in the morning and afternoon. We would go on break immediately. Some of us would walk out on the railroad tracks a ways to have a smoke. Smoking wasn't allowed inside the fence for obvious reasons. We would often go in the machine shop to get out of the sun and go to the bathroom. When the boss (Jensen?) would come down there in his green panel truck, we would wait until he pulled up on the far side of the building and then run out the side door. I saw others doing that, one day, from my vantage point in the shade on the steps of a tank. Two guys tried to get out at the same time and got stuck in the door. It slowed the process down so much that one of them only got a few feet before he felt he had to look busy so he bent over a 12 inch pipe and gave it a rap with his big pipe wench. He wasn't within 20 feet of a valve where the wrench could be used.

Cutting weeds was done by hand with a long handled grass razor. It was not hard work but monotonous. It also ruined my golf game. I didn't know that until a year later because I didn't play golf that year. Spending 8 hours on the grass each day seems like enough. When I next tried to golf I had a terrible duck hook from swinging that grass razor with my right wrist. It was something I never was able to correct completely.

John and I used to sit on the steps of a tank and sharpen our grass razors with a sharpening stone. Sitting down felt so good that we had really sharp razors. Sometimes we would just hold the stone in position in case Jensen would come around the corner. He was sneaky that way. He caught us once and said he had been watching us for ten minutes and we hadn't moved. It was a good thing he didn't know we were there for an hour without moving.

Jensen was easy to dislike. He pretended to know everything. We got a new type of 50 gal. drum-mover and he decided to demonstrate it for us in a safety meeting. The drums were very heavy and contained the additives that were put into gasoline there. One was called TCP. Jensen was a small man and had been told that this newly designed drum mover was better because it would balance the weight when the drum was tipped. The problem came when Jensen tried to set it back in its upright position. It went in a hurry and took him with it. He flew right over the top of the drum. We enjoyed that safety meeting more than any other.

Sometimes we used mowing equipment with gasoline engines. We called one 'old shaky' because the handlebars would shake back and forth to counteract the cycle bar's action.

The tanks were connected with pipes for filling and draining but they were also connected by pipes that held vapor. Every third or fourth tank had a top that would rise and fall with this vapor pressure. We heard a hissing of this vapor at a joint one time and reported it. Gasoline vapors were worse than the liquid and could have exploded when we went through it with our power equipment. It surprised us that this repair was given the three-day priority like everything else. After that we knew we were on own for safety in spite of the meetings and propaganda. Most days were too hot that summer. In the fall some were too cold. I've never been as cold as I was one day when a wind was blowing a cold drizzle in my face and I wasn't dressed for it.

I didn't mind going back to school that fall but not until John and I took a three-day trip up north.

We left after work since his car was already packed with the tent, sleeping bags, and whatever we decided to take. We got as far as the first bar and stopped for a cold one. After that we felt we were on vacation and went quite a ways north before we found another bar. This time we stayed too long. When we left we felt like singing so we sang *Good Night Irene* for the next 50 miles. By then it was dark and raining. We had no particular destination in mind so we decided to make camp in a grassy area next to the road. Putting up the tent in the rain was hard since one of us had to be inside holding it up while the other put in corner stakes. The ground was so soft that the stakes wound pull out each time the tent was pulled to one side or the other. This was happening because the one inside was a little dizzy trying to stand in the dark. We finally got it to stand but not straight. We were both wet and either didn't have rain gear or forgot to put it on. I had a dark blue sweater on that turned my white shirt all blue. I took them both off and threw them in the corner of the tent. My sleeping bag was dry and it felt good because it was fairly cold that September night. I woke up once during the night and noticed water running through the tent. I was all right but it was getting John wet so I woke him. He moved over a little bit and went back to sleep. In the morning we were awakened by a car stopping and someone saying, "My God, look at that." When we got up we could see the problem. We were camped in the bottom of a ditch with water running through it. Worse than that the car was on the side of the ditch leaning at an awkward angle. We weren't sure it would stay upright when we got into it. We flipped a coin to see who would drive it out and who would push. It came out without trouble.

John knew of a resort where he had gone as a kid so we headed there. They rented boats so we got one. I had brought my Dad's outboard motor and John knew of an uninhabited island not too far away. We set up camp there and went fishing. It was a windy day and the waves were high enough that the motor would come out of the water between each wave. It would rev up and slow down in a rhythmic way. John caught a nice northern but I don't remember how we cleaned it or cooked it.

We found some nice bars in the neighborhood for our evening entertainment. We met a couple of girls at one but they were already with guys so they invited us to come to their work the next day. They worked at a swanky resort that served dinners on the American plan so they said they could get a couple of extras for us. We went up the back stairs and sure enough, they delivered two lobster-tail dinners to us on a big platter. We ate the lobster (first time I had ever eaten it) and threw the empty dishes in the lake off the end of the dock just as we had been instructed to do. Later when the girls got off work, we went to our island where we had prepared a huge log pile for a fire. It sounds like a movie but we just talked half the night and then took them home. I don't think we saw them again. We explored a lot of the lake by boat and some of the countryside by car before we went home and back to school.

Trips out of town were rare. I went with Jo to her home in Balaton a few times. I also went to see John Baker in Ames Iowa where he attended medical school. I sat in on some of his classes and went out with some nurses. Nurses were more than anxious to go out with medical students and even paid for the beer. John lived in a room in the YMCA. I also went to see Dave Nielsen at St. Olaf and saw how he lived in a fraternity house. They both looked good compared to my living at home.

Senior Year

During my senior year I found I was short two required courses, political science and sociology. Somehow I got the same instructor for both. His last name was Ransom and the kids called him Hansom Ransom. I don't know why. He talked a mile a minute and sometimes developed spit on his lower lip that he would eventually suck back in. Someone said he had been a Rhodes Scholar. That might have been true. At least I know he had a vocabulary like no one else I had heard. I, of course, hated both of these courses and did what I could to point this out. First of all, the words *political* and *science* should not be in the same sentence let alone side by side. They stand for complete opposites.

There were three of us in the sociology class that

kept asking embarrassing questions. One of the others was Bob Cummings and I can't remember who the third one was. Bob became a physician in Minneapolis and I saw him a few years later.

One day I told Ransom that he was contradicting something he had said the day before and I pointed to my notes. He came down the isle to look at my notes and found he couldn't read them. He said, "I can't read them." I said, "It's because I took them with my left hand." He said, Aren't you left handed?" and I said, "No, I decided to learn how to write with my left hand so that this hour wouldn't be a complete waste." That was the kind of dialog that we had until the final.

The final was something to remember. Actually I took two of them from him. The first one was in Political Science and it was in the morning. It was all true or false. The exam was about ten pages long and with his vocabulary it was hard enough to understand the questions let alone know the answers. It was mostly guessing on my part. After the two-hour exam we were turning in our tests and I overheard him say to a couple of his pets, "How many did you think were true?" Then the answer came back, "Most of them." At that point he told them they were all true. I was trying to remember if I had even a majority of them true. I remembered this in the afternoon when I was taking the Sociology test. It too was true or false and I couldn't understand the questions. After about five minutes I decided that they could all be true so I put a T at the top of each page and drew an arrow to the bottom and turned it in. They were all true and I had a perfect test. He wasn't amused, however, and gave me a D in the course. I didn't ask him how he determined that. I didn't want to see him again. Years later I was with my brother in Mankato and went to the Century Club for a drink. Ransom was there sitting alone at the bar so I went up to him and said, "I think I should have had an A in that course." He spun around on his stool and started sputtering at me like it had been yesterday. My brother got a big bang out of it.

I sold Cutco Cutlery door-to-door my senior year in addition to everything else. We had a boss who taught us the ropes and took a percentage of the sales. They were good knives but expensive and therefore hard to sell. The cheapest knife was $5 or $6 and the big sets were over $100.

We were taught many sales tricks. One of them involved asking to see the knives that the prospective customer was using at the time. We then ran one across our thumb to show that it wasn't sharp. This worked fine until I did it for Jo's sister. She had a sharp serrated knife that cut right into my thumb.

I set up shop in a girls dorm and sold many sets because they could be bought on monthly payments. I would wave part of my commission to cover the down payment and would be paid the rest when the knives had been completely paid and delivered. The problem was that no one ever got them paid off.

I went out in the country and tried to sell them to farmers. They always let me in and let me give my entire sales pitch but never bought any knives.

I gave away little green bud vases to everyone that let me in for a sales pitch. I see them at garage sales today and have purchased 8 or 10 of them.

My senior year was relatively easy but I was anxious to graduate. I had already completed most of the science courses. I took a year of advanced calculus but it was quite easy. By now, Jo had caught up to me and we took it together. We did many homework problems together at Paul's. I was reminded that I had said that I would help her if she majored in math but now she was mostly helping me.

We had Hatfield for an instructor and that was a let down from Walter Fleming who was head of the department and had taught us calculus. I spent too much time correcting Hatfield and it was pointed out to me that his eye would point outward whenever I raised my hand.

It was a mistake to compare other instructors to

Fleming because he was exceptionally good. I did it anyway and felt we deserved the best.

Fleming planned each lecture down to the minute and wasted no time. He was very meticulous as he drew things on the board. He drew beautiful coordinate systems with triangles, ellipses, circles, sign waves, and other math functions. I spent a lot of time watching him teach so I could emulate him someday (I thought at that point that I would end up teaching math at some level someday). I took no notes so I had to pay attention to the things that he said.

He was my favorite teacher but didn't stay at T.C. long and they didn't name any buildings after him. As a matter of fact he wasn't treated very well by the administration because he didn't have his degrees in education. He actually was a mathematician. This showed me that T.C. was more interested in making a teacher an expert in teaching without caring if they knew their subject very well.

I got nearly all A's in math and got the "Outstanding Math Grad" award. I liked that and felt I was justified in my negative attitude toward other courses. It was a pretty narrow view, however. Jo also had mostly A's in math and went on to teach it.

Organic Qual (qualitative analysis) was reportedly the toughest of all the chemistry classes so I waited until my senior year to take it. We were given 5 unknown solutions and were suppose to find out what they were and then make a derivative which is a known crystalline compound made from it that had a certain melting point which would confirm the finding. We were suppose to use all of our previous knowledge of chemistry to do this. The fact that we were given 5 unknowns presented a big challenge. There were hundreds of tests that could be used to narrow down the possibilities until the true one was found. To make it even harder, there was only a small amount of solution to start with and each test would consume some. Fortunately I had an edge. When I was taking physical chemistry, Dr. Ford received a war surplus Dipping Refractometer. He asked me to unpack it, check it out, and write a procedure for using it. It turned out to be a wonderfully accurate devise that would give the index of refraction of a chemical as accurately as the book on indexes of refraction. Perhaps they were a part of the *Chemical Rubber Tables.* Anyway, I used this new instrument to identify 4 of the 5 unknowns the first day. The fifth was a mixture and took the rest of the quarter to solve. Making the derivatives was not easy either but I got them all to melt at the right temperature.

I soon realized that I would have to go to graduate school before I could get a job since I didn't take the education courses that I would have needed to become a high school teacher. With that in mind, I looked for a beginning course in German to take knowing that a foreign language was needed for most master's degrees in science. I found one called elementary German 103. Mrs. Vilhelmine Kaufmanis taught the course. I went to class with some trepidation because I had no experience in a foreign language. She started class by taking roll and then handed out the text we would use. It looked interesting to me because it was a story about Einstein and his theories written in German. After she handed out the text she said, "Lesen sie bitte mein Herr Lagerquist." I recognized my name so I said, "What?" She then said I don't remember you being in our class the last two quarters when we took 101 and 102. What a goof I had made. I should have figured that out before I signed up. I told her I had made a mistake and told her why I had wanted a start in German. When I offered to drop the class, she said, "Not yet. Let's see what we can do with this." She stayed after class each day so I could read to her and I picked up on the different way they used their verbs. I thought it was a good idea. I memorized many words and eventually got an A in the class. A few years later I passed an exam in chemical German for my master's degree in chemical engineering. Mrs. Kaufmanis was one of the rare ones.

Her husband was a professor at Gustavus and in our senior year came to T.C. to teach astronomy that I had previously taken from Hatfield. Jo had astronomy from Kaufmanis and said he was very good.

There were other good professors that Jo had and told me about like Paul, Lokensgard, and Emma Wiecking. She also had some that were bad like the one that taught music appreciation. How can anyone screw up a course that deals with listening to good music? I took it too but can't remember who taught it to me.

There were lots of social functions and many extra curriculum activities available. I played softball for the chemistry team in the intramural league. We went to all the home football games, basketball games, and dances afterward. The science fair was something I liked and helped out with each year. There were many clubs and I belonged to a couple of them (like Sigma Zeta which was a national science honor society) but can't remember what they did except to pose for the picture to put in the Annual.

When I looked back at the Annuals for these years I was surprised to see so many of our teachers were classified as instructors. Many of them did not have their PhD. There were also some assistant professors but few associate professors. Only department heads were full professors. Even Fleming was only an associate professor because the math 'department' was a part of the science department. Later I was an instructor and then an assistant professor at the University of Minnesota so I know the feeling of being at the bottom of the academic ladder.

I had very little respect for T.C. while I was going there and felt it was not up to the academic standards I thought it ought to be. The truth is that I probably wasn't ready for anything of a higher standard anyway. I wasn't ready to give up any of my enjoyment time for hard study. There were times when I felt like doing the work and getting caught up. When I did it I felt good but it never lasted. There were too many fun things to do. I was lucky that I went to T.C.

After T.C. I went to graduate school and found standards that were so high that I wasn't ready for them. Physics was a good example. I had to drop graduate courses in physics at the University of Washington and take senior level courses. Even they were hard work. At that point I felt my criticism of T.C. was justified.

I majored in math, physics, and chemistry without working hard and finished in four years. That wouldn't have been possible in most schools. I learned how to get by rather than mastering the subject. This was a mistake but came in handy later in life when I had jobs that could not be done completely by one person in the time I was given. I did them without getting frustrated because I had experience doing it.

Growing Up

I can't think of a better place to grow up or a better time than Mankato, Minnesota in the 30's and 40's. Not only for the things we had, but the things we didn't have. We didn't have traffic problems, crime, shootings, smog, drugs, obesity, or gangs. We had the run of the town at all hours without worry. These times were marked by the lack of change. No new houses were built (except a few basement houses with the promise of a top later). Even the new German Lutheran Church was started with a basement. No new businesses were started and none of the old ones failed. No new roads or bridges were built. Mankato High School wasn't even replaced until after I had graduated. It was a strange time but one that we came to accept as normal. When millions of young men went off to war it left a big void in the work force at home. Women, older men, and younger kids filled this void. We were expected to grow up faster than we ordinarily would have because of this. Those that went to war became known as the greatest generation. Their kids that were born after the war were to become known as the baby boomers. We were in between and had no generation identity. Even 'our' war in Korea was called a police action. To the 95% of the boys in my high school class that went into the service, it was a war not deserving of any dignifying names. One of my classmates was the first Minnesotan to be killed there. His name was Terry Haskell to us but on the memorial stone in Mankato his first name is listed as Beverly. Maybe that's why he was known as Terry. I guess we should be called the forgotten generation. In a way, that's all right. We didn't seek notoriety or wish to change the world. We were industrious and well behaved but independently minded. We thought we were entitled to an opinion but didn't believe in civil disobedience to get our way. That came later and we despised it.

During this time when hardly anything changed, women's skirt lengths went up and down like a yo-yo. Not only that but all the women conformed to the style of the moment. I couldn't understand this and often asked my mother why didn't the women revolt. Men's clothes changed some, too, but we always had a chance to wear out the old style while the new styles came into acceptance.

Growing up is a slow process that is mostly waiting. Waiting for the next good thing that will come, whether it is a watch, a bike, a girl, a job, or moving out of the house. One doesn't get a new brain and become grown up. Instead, a new outlook that is based on all that has gone before emerges. It is coupled with a desire to have your own family without giving up the old one entirely while the priority slowly switches away from the security of someone else's family to your own. I was ready to move out after high school but there wasn't enough money to send me out of town to college. I knew I had to go to college so I could get a job that wasn't all physical labor. I had seen enough of that already. So I waited again but this time I knew who I was going to live with and that made it a little easier. Jo and I have been married 46 years and have 4 wonderful kids.

Even after the flood I stayed active in the Boy Scout's Order of the Arrow program. I was Master of Ceremonies at a dinner once at the Century Club in the Summer of 1951.

I was 41 when my dad died and it wasn't nearly as painful as if it had happened while I lived at home. I still have his shotgun and .22 but haven't fired them since he died.

My mother is 95 and lives in a nursing home in Minnesota. She remembers me but often doesn't remember my visits the day after I leave.

Bill managed and owned several businesses in Mankato before he retired and moved to Arkansas.

Ann married Al Fero and lives in Hamel, Minnesota, where she has been able to help care for our mother.

Jimmy Nielsen became known as David when he went to college at St. Olaf because that was his first name. His dad's name was also David so while he lived at home he was Jimmy. I think he preferred Jim. He became a medical doctor like he said he would partly because his mother had died of cancer.

John Baker also became a doctor. He was an Osteopath and practiced in Colorado where we got reacquainted.

Lin Barnes recently completed 12 years as a County Commissioner in Blue Earth County after managing the North-Star Concrete Plant that I so fondly remember.

Ken Uhlhorn became a professor at Indiana State University and still lives near there. He married Harriet Sexe who was a year behind us in school.

Phil Cowan became a Forest Ranger in Yellowstone National Park. I heard he was still a firefighter after he turned 60.

Jim Taylor got a PhD. and has written 20 books on business management. He has been a visiting professor in 7 countries and is list in Who's Who.

Mary Meyer retired as Dean of the College of Applied Sciences at Western Illinois University. Her husband, John Leach, was also a Dean there. She has a street named for her in the new part of North Mankato on top of Belgrade hill. It is called Mary Lane. It is off of James Drive (named for her brother) near Meyer Court (the family name).

Marilyn Phillipson (Skip) married Jimmy's (now Dave's) brother, Roger Nielsen. After running several businesses in southern Minnesota, they moved to Arizona.

Donna Norlund married Gordon Holmgren and has lived near Mankato until they retired and moved to northern Minnesota. He was one of the kids in my conformation class.

Julie Williams married a Navy pilot, Ted Miller, and came back to Mankato to live after his service.

Dolly Overlie married George Carlstrom, a local contractor, another member of my conformation class.

Karen Oversea married Ken Prihoda and lives in Hutchinson where he was a teacher.

Harriet McDonald married Jack Kent, who was two years ahead of us in school, and now lives in Florida.

Dick Ryan was in line to go to a military academy but a shotgun accident took one of his feet. He now owns a bookstore in Steamboat Springs, Colorado and rides his bike across the country for sport.

Kathleen Lundin married Bob Beck and lives in a western suburb of Minneapolis.

Al LaFrance and Stan Cooper live in Florida and North Carolina and I see them only briefly at High School reunions.

Corky lived a long life and died peacefully while I lived with my family and had my own dog.

My grandma died 5 years after Grandpa died.

Uncle Irving, Aunt Rufine and Janice (Lagerquist) Broen are dead.

Many of my friends of my youth mentioned here are dead, as well. Some are; Bob Imm, Trish Imm, Jon Nordgren, Janet Flitter, Myrn Swanson, John Kolling, Lloyd Horness, Bob Apple, Terry Haskell, Don Wyland, Ken Beavens, Hal Bohrer, Rick Bohrer, Dave Eilenfeldt, David Sweiger and Tom Boyce.

I talked to my 6th grade teacher, Virginia Rettke Charlton, on the phone recently. She didn't remember me but enjoyed talking about those years.

I have talked a couple of times to my high school teacher, John Larson, in his hometown of Hackensack, Minn.

I found out that Hildegarde Horeni was living in Santa Fe in 2000 so I called her on the phone and eventually went to see her. She didn't remember me but was just as nice as she had been in school.

We contacted Walter Fleming in 1999 and got him to come to our lake cabin for a few days. We all enjoyed that very much.

I occasionally correspond with or talk to my junior high teachers, Ivan Underdahl and Betty Morphew. Ivan lives in a western suburb of Minneapolis and supplied me with information on Norway when I told him we were going there for a visit. The information included a picture of him in front of the general store in Undredal, Norway where his relatives originated. Betty lives in Tucson, Ariz. She said she enjoyed an earlier version of this book but remembers some things a little differently. I wonder what she meant by that.

As for me, I haven't grown up yet.

I still play golf but gave up bowling. I have Grandpa's wallet, shotgun, and two handsaws. I still use the handsaws.

Descendants of Claus August Lagerquist

1. Claus August Lagerquist (b.1873;d.1945)
  sp: Betsy Nelson (b.1874;m.1899;d.1949)
   2. Kenneth Nelson Lagerquist (b.1902,d.1974)
    sp: Florence Gertrude Christensen (b.1906;m.1929)
    3. William Burton Lagerquist (b.1930)
       sp: Alice Ruth Rohlik (b.1929;m.1955;d.1978)
       4. Steven James Lagerquist (b.1960)
          sp: Ronnita (m.(Div))
           5. Chelsea Lea Lagerquist (b.1984)
           5. Melyse Renay Lagerquist (b.1986)
           5. Ethan Emerson Lagerquist (b.1987)
            sp: Kayla Lynn (m.1991)
           5. Alyson Faith Lagerquist (b.1994)
           5. Kaylyn Karissa Lagerquist (b.1996)
       4. David William Lagerquist (b.1962)
         sp: Pauline (b.1962)
           5. Austin Lagerquist (b.1993)
           5. Jessica Lagerquist (b.1997)
           5. Callie Marie Lagerquist (b.1999)
       4. Michael Scott Lagerquist (b.1962)
    3. Clayton Ross Lagerquist (b.1933)
       sp: Amy Joanne Larson (b.1934;m.1955)
       4. Jon William Lagerquist (b.1956)
          sp: Arlene Catherine Young (b.1958;m.1978)
           5. Jon William Lagerquist, Jr. (b.1980)
           5. Jason Ross Lagerquist (b.1983)
       4. Eric Olaf Lagerquist (b.1961)
       4. Carrie Jean Lagerquist (b.1964)
          sp: Mark Vogt (b.1962,m.1984(Div))
           5. Kyle Blaine Vogt (b.1987)
           5. Cameron Michael Vogt (b.1989)
       4. Gail Ann Lagerquist (b.1967)
          sp: Gerald Francis Nygaard (b.1967;m.1996)
           5. Mitchell James Nygaard (b.1998)
           5. Tristan Jack Nygaard (b.2001)

    3. Ann Florence Lagerquist (b.1939)
      sp: Alan Fero (b.1931;m.1977)
  2. Irving Carl Lagerquist (b.1907;d.1979)
      sp: Rufine Klawitter (b.1910;m.1933;d.1990)
    3. Janice Caryn Lagerquist (b.1938;d.1986)
    sp: Donald Broen (b.1937;m.1960)
      4. Kimberly Caryn Broen (b.1964)
      4. Cheryl Kristyn Broen (b.1967)

Photographs